COLLINS GUIDE
TO WILD HABITATS

WOODLANDS-
DECIDUOUS

Horse Chestnut candles

COLLINS GUIDE TO WILD HABITATS

CHRIS PACKHAM

With 56 colour photographs
by the author and 5 colour
plates by Chris Shields

LEFT **Feather on bark**

COLLINS
Grafton Street

WOODLANDS ~DECIDUOUS

This book is for His Excellency
Maximilian de Barstardos,
Emperor of Midanbury.

William Collins Sons & Co Ltd
London · Glasgow · Sydney · Auckland
Toronto · Johannesburg
Text and photographs © 1989 Chris Packham
Colour plates © 1989 Chris Shields

First Edition 1989

Designer: Caroline Hill

ISBN 0 00 219841 X Paperback
ISBN 0 00 219867 3 Hardback

Filmset by Ace Filmsetting Ltd, Frome,
Somerset
Colour origination by
Wace Litho, Birmingham, UK
Printed and bound by
New Interlitho SpA, Milan, Italy

CONTENTS

The end of years of life

Acknowledgements are due to: John Buckley, for telling me not to collect birds eggs and pin butterflies; Graham Hirons and Andrew Parfitt for access to their knowledge; to Andrew Welch and Nicholas Yeats for endless abuse; to Barbara Levy for yet more compassionate tolerance; and especially to Stephen 'I had to have it' Bolwell, the greatest collector who ever lived; to my father's wellingtons; to my mother; to the Prettiest Star; to the Tiny Twinkleheart; and to Jenny for synergism.

ACKNOWLEDGEMENTS

LEFT **A towering beech tree**

Summer. There's a droning dirge of insects buzzing as if there's a giant swarm becoming monotonously frenzied somewhere. Yet there is no swarm. There is no single insect immediately visible other than a few hungry flies on my forearm. It must be the sound of ten thousand hoverflies loafing in the leafiness which has enveloped me. A Spotted Flycatcher busies itself from its perch on the end of a tortured oak bough. He sits silently, still except for the twisting of his head, and then at random he jump-jets into the canopy in a short sally to snatch one of the invisible millions. Back to the perch. Head-turn, head-turn, head-turn, over-wing scratch, sally, snatch. Back to perch. For half an hour. What a life of pale yellow and pallid green shade with a dash of activity!

Beneath him Redstarts dapple-flash like broken fireworks and then flinch uncontrollably on mossy branches, their mouths crammed with an untidy, leggy wreckage of the insect nation. The male is resplendent in his avant-garde attire of black, grey and white, while the female is a sensible brown still tipped with that Redstart flag of brick red tail. Flit, flinch, flutter, flash, feed.

From the right the droning intensifies and the mellow yellow yields a mustard-tempered soldier of misfortune. Initially the furious humming surrounds you, your early warning systems overwhelmed in this glade. But then you catch a glimpse of your target. He's moving fast, skirting the bracken landscape with a mad intention, buzzing in broad banks and shallow curves. A vespid attack-ship with fire in his compound eyes. A black-banded soldier from an errorless social system. So arrogant, this Hornet, smart in his art-deco uniform, militaristic in a Viennese style. He shoots past the flycatcher and zips after the Redstart into the shade, flashing like a radar blip, a stinging sunspot through the

LEFT **A gossamer duet: a dandelion and a lacewing**
RIGHT **A Tawny Owl**

9

dapples until he buzzes away. Honey-suckle drips honey for the bumble bees to hive, and a gang of butterflies frolics about. Speckled Woods, White Admirals and Silver-washed Fritillaries smother the terraced columns of spiked yellow, white and pink flowers, as it ascends into the high canopy upwards to the free air of the outside world.

If you could put your ear to the stem of the Bracken, like a Red Indian's to a railway line, you'd hear a probing, gasping and bubbling as a tiny midge sucks fluid from the plant's canals. His fluffy antennae, feathery tufts, are probably more sensitive than every nerve cell in your body lined end to end. Suddenly he flinches and pulls hard at his tiny, sucking stylet, twisting and tugging it out of its fleshy meal. His wings vibrate. There's a female about somewhere, probably about two hundred metres away, and he's off to find her with an army of other males in the area as rival suitors. It's like you chasing after a mate who is in Siberia with the whole of London as your competition. Quite ridiculous. Still, he's gone, and now the Bracken weeps a little amber fluid from its wound. But before you can get off your knees another member of the myriad millions arrives to drink it. This little red-eyed fly feeds using a clubbed proboscis, which thumps down like a fisted arm punching a carpet. At each stab the pool gets smaller until only a tiny stain remains and the fly vanishes. The flycatcher's head turns. Head turns. Sally. Snatch. Perch.

Only yards away a Fallow Deer's tail swings metronomically over its rump, a diagrammatic cushion of black and white, constantly keeping the insect millions moving on. At the other end of this ungulate tube, black lips covered in a down of soft, sensitive hairs search feverishly for nutrient-rich fodder. Simply by design she knows just that leaf, of that age, on that plant which holds the phosphorus, calcium, manganese, iron or nitrogen; this is no random meal. It's a fixed menu for fitness, a survival salad for Fallow does and fawns, served fresh for tactile tongues and elegant ladies with smooth, oval necks and languid legs. Aloof on the hoof. Not my favourites, deer always appear like snobs with little interest or intelligence, capitalistically guarding their clique herds and pieces of woodland.

Far off a Green Woodpecker laughs raucously and I wonder if the woodpecker's life is as easy as the flycatcher's appears. I suppose that somewhere the woodpeckers are murdering more of the insect millions for woodpeckerets, who are caged in a sweaty, stinking hole, sticking together, tangling up their feather-pins, getting bad-tempered, playing Trotsky with their ice-pick beaks and making loud and vulgar noises. Meanwhile the male woodpecker is either kicking its way into a hard ants' nest somewhere or poking around in some damp ground while the female woodpecker is probably lazing behind a tree, preening.

I take two steps and I am in yet another woodland world. I turn in despair because I have got just a month to write all this down. It was a Ladybird book 110 million years ago in the time of the first few trees, at the Observer's book stage when more than fifty species had evolved, has passed through the Britannica edition and is now beyond the scope of the whole British Library. I've missed my chance; God should have written this book at the beginning, when it was shorter.

Let me spoil this book and tell you the climax of the story first. This will save you reading it backwards and put a few of the complexities into perspective by initiating some questions which the following chapter will answer.

Deciduous woodland is the seral climax vegetation over much of modern Europe. That is to say, that without man's interference it is what most of Europe should be covered in and, if left alone, what most parts would eventually revert to. Not that too much remains, however, but there is sure to be a fragment of an ecosystem dominated by deciduous hardwood trees, in one of their many permutations and combinations, somewhere within your reach. It is simply the most diverse, most complex, most species-rich and most precious habitat that carpets our particular part of the planet; the most exciting, if not the most frustrating of habitats.

THE SPARROWHAWK

The climax. A sunny day in May. I slid down a shallow bank under some oaks into a bath of green. I was drowned in a living light machine. A human intrusion into the process of photosynthesis. The expanse of wet Bracken soaked my torso and the woods soaked my mind. There was no sky and no ground. I was, it seemed, suspended in all of that spatial complexity, swimming in Bracken through a huge emerald cathedral whose buttresses were living boughs, whose windows were ten million living leaves. I felt the triumph and turned round and round. About fifty metres on I began to struggle, my feet faltered over fallen branches and amongst obscured rabbit holes. Sweat from the struggle began to line my waterproofs and rapidly my rejoicing was reversed. A madness set in, an insane claustrophobia. By now I could taste the woodland in my mouth. Chiffchaffs were not singing but yelling in the huge, dangerous oaks. It was a belligerent panic. I hated Bracken and strode into it like a giant into lesser men, striking and hacking. I hated the greenness, the wetness and the smell. As I got clear of the Bracken on a steep slope under some birches I could see space, but then had to claw through some wicked birch brashings. Thin, black, whippy twigs, slapping and stinging as savage as barbed wire. Panting, I reached a woodland clearing, feeling like I had escaped from a war. In the glade nothing moved except me, the sole survivor.

Brilliant sunshine punctured the trees and made me squint painfully after the spangled shade of the interior. Here the grass was very, very green, the sky very, very blue. I froze, feeling alien, and listened to the aftermath of my battle through the trees. Ferns snapped and flicked about spasmodically, green shadows lost in the dinginess. I turned to look into the clearing and saw three large oak trees. Nothing. Then I looked at my binoculars. Full of debris and soaking wet. Then I looked up again and it started. Seven seconds of magical action.

A brown bird appeared out of the woods at the other end of the clearing. It flashed cream and dropped to ground level by two thorn shrubs. It then flew along the entire length of the clearing, about one metre off the ground; an almost invisible sliver of feathers. Like a bullet. Like a guided missile. A weapon without error, designed by the woods from which it had come. The contours of the ground brought it towards me in a shallow curve, until it was coming straight for me. Suddenly, small bird, mauve, bullfinch. Two birds, explosion, sound. Empty clearing.

Had it happened? Was it a warp in time, a hiccup? If I had blinked twice I would have missed it. I stood perplexed until the dream fractured. Dancing in the Maytime was a small white feather from the finch's rump. That was the climax. It was there because of the soft, musty humus, the myriads of opalescent springtails, the beetles, the Bracken, the Badgers, the tits, the transpiration, the photosynthesis, the trophic levels, the nutrient cycles, the complexity of the community. It was basically because of the trees. Millions and millions of tonnes of wood, thousands of years of seral development and hundreds of thousands of years of life in southern England had all paid off. The Sparrowhawk had killed. The efficiency was devastating, a triumph of evolution, a pinnacle of predation, and I was a witness. When I was fourteen I didn't know how it had worked, I had never even heard of community complexity, ecosystems or trophisms, but I now had to find out. Some Swallows twittered in the blue and I disappeared from the sunlight under an historic oak and back into the woodlands.

MATERIALS AND MECHANICS

It is fifteen million degrees Celsius in the heart of our star, the sun, a nuclear fireball one and a half million miles in diameter, a primitive, chemical hell of hydrogen and helium pumping and bubbling on the mega-scale. It is not and then it is. A massless elementary particle, named a photon by Everyman's definition of a genius, Albert Einstein, is created in the core of the sun. It moves out through the brilliancy of the photosphere, the yellow so hot it's white, into the cooler corona, a mere million degrees, then it and its tiny unit, or quanta, of energy leaves the sun at 300,000 kilometres per second, outpacing the solar winds into space. Whether it is corpuscular or waving energy is meaningless to us all. It is red light. Twice as fast as blue light and a mere sliver of the spectrum which fascinated Newton, Einstein and Maxwell.

Meanwhile, ninety-three million miles away on a pretty little blue planet a leaf twitches in a warm sunny breeze, a complex of tissues packed with the chemical engineering that lets the little blue planet breathe and the mechanisms to take a few basic organic ingredients such as carbon dioxide and water and weave them into complex molecules. It seems amazing that such a simple thing is able to nourish itself. Autotrophy from just a leaf!

But now, 8.3 seconds later, it arrives, careering through space, passing instantaneously the tiny burned coal of Mercury, the searing acid clouds of Venus, and the satellite we call the Moon, speeding down through the ozone layer through a crack in the clouds, narrowly missing the shimmering wing of a Swallow which skirts the tree, before smashing into the leaf. Now we're in the micro–minuto scale. It zooms through the waterproof cuticle, passes the leaf skin or epidermis and streaks into the palisade cells which form the bulk of the leaf tissue.

LEFT **A Lime Hawkmoth**
RIGHT **Hazel catkins rich in pollen**

2. THE LIGHT FACTORY

On through the web of cellulose molecules that make up the cell wall, into the cell cytoplasm and through the double membrane that encapsulates the crux of its goal. Gone now are a trillion of its colleagues. Some got lost seven seconds ago in the solar winds, others were reflected off the clouds back into space, and a few billion gave the blue beauty to the iridescence of the Swallow's wings a millionth of a second ago. It dies now, crashing into one of the many thyllakoids, sheets of tissue holding green coloured discs called grana inside a single structural unit – the chloroplast. It is on the surface of one of these membranes, deep inside a smaller unit called a quantasome, that it collides with a porphyrin molecule called chlorophyll. Lured by chlorophyll's magnesium core, its welcome is dramatic. The whole molecule is excited for a minute fraction of time during which the photon gives up its energy to the photochemical process of photosynthetic phosphorylation. This photon's energy causes electrons to dance from one chlorophyll molecule to another. Eventually, the chlorophyll molecule becomes unstable and splits a water molecule into hydrogen and oxygen. The oxygen is the waste, for us all to breathe, while the hydrogen is used to reduce carbon dioxide to a sugar, which in turn is converted into carbohydrates, fats, proteins and all the numerous complex molecules built around carbon. These are then used in the building of plant tissue, which in turn provides the food for the 5–10 million species of animals, or heterotrophs, who cannot synthesize their own molecules. So without plants our little blue planet could not be the living Earth. The scales involved are awe-inspiring. The single hottest entity in the solar system gives rise to the fastest particle, which makes all of our world work by tickling minuscule molecules inside the cells of leaves.

ANNUAL PRODUCTION

Each quantasome contains 230 chlorophyll molecules and there may be hundreds of thousands of quantasomes on each of the sixty granal discs found in each unit chloroplast. Within an oak leaf palisade cell there may be 200 chloroplasts and each leaf may have 25 million palisade cells, giving a total of 500 million chloroplasts in each leaf. There may be 200 million oak leaves in one hectare of woodland spreading a total of 6 kilogrammes of chlorophyll over 8 hectares of leaf area and in one year these units will fix 10,000 kilogrammes of carbon into sugars, fats or proteins. Thus each tree is a machine for trapping light and woodland as a whole can be regarded as a light factory where each species, each individual, is struggling desperately to maximize its input.

The results of this intense competition for light can be seen in the great diversity of plant life within the woodland and the way in which the plant community has developed a stratified structure best suited to utilize the solar energy.

FACTORY DESIGN

Woodland is not flat or planar, like heathland, downland or a beach, it is under your feet and above your head, and if you don't look where you are going, on the end of your nose! You walk ON a heath but IN a wood. It envelops a space of about 2 million cubic metres per hectare, a spongy layer over the surface of the earth where you can stumble through the airholes. Thus it has a greater structural complexity than any other habitat, and, of course, the academics have gone to their categorizing with relish.

Trees taller than 10 metres form what the botanists call the main storey. Beneath this is the under storey, consisting of young individuals of the dominant species or smaller trees like Hazel *Corylus avellana*, Hawthorn *Crataegus monogyna* or Holly *Ilex aquifolium*. The shrub layer comprises woody shrubs which are too shaded by the upper storey to grow taller, and beneath these there is a dwarf-shrub layer of woody species less than 0.5 metre

The thick carpet of vegetation under a hazel coppice

high such as Brambles *Rubus fruticosus* and Heather *Calluna vulgaris*. The tall herb layer is composed of species more than a metre tall, such as Nettles *Urtica dioica*, and Foxgloves *Digitalis purpurea*, and beneath these are the smaller non-woody plants, including Bluebells *Hyacinthoides non-scriptus*, Daffodils *Narcissus pseudo-narcissus*, Ramsons *Allium ursinum* and Dog's Mercury *Mercurialis perennis*. Lastly there is the ground layer typified by liverworts, mosses, the *Bryophyta*, and similar plants, such as ferns, which grow on the floor itself.

Within this scientific separation none of the plants simply exist side-by-side. Each of the species is involved in a complex of interactions with other species, and the whole woodland is a product of something far beyond the sum of its component parts. It is a community with characteristics and

properties of its own, and yet this is still not what we should call woodland.

The climate, temperature, wind, moisture, soil type, subsoil type, the chemical nature of the soil and degree of exposure, to a large extent limits which organisms can survive in any particular system. For any set of environmental conditions there is a characteristic set of dominant plant species which may occupy the area. Once established, the plants themselves modify the environment, providing shelter, humidity pockets, shade, etc. and create suitable conditions for the second series of dependent plant species. Associated with this spectrum of plants will be a set of herbivorous animals whose food species are present, and associated with these will be a particular set of carnivores which prey on those herbivores and so on through the web of the ecosystem.

15

Autumn larch and Bracken

THE FUNCTIONAL SYSTEM

It is this assemblage that is woodland. It is a whole ecosystem comprising many communities of organisms. It is independent, self-contained and self-sufficient. The biological relationships between members of the woodland ecosystem are many and varied. One animal may rely on one plant or another animal for its habitat, either for feeding, hiding, breeding or sleeping. Relationships may be more intimate, such as plants relying on insects for their pollination and on mammals and birds for the dispersal of their seeds. Plants and animals may compete amongst themselves for food and shelter, and it is this competition which shapes the entire ecosystem, and gives it its great diversity of life. The scope for diversity is provided by the producers, the autotrophic plants in the ecosystem that are able to produce energy from sunlight and are thus self-sufficient. The consumers are heterotrophic, needing to derive their energy from the

producers or each other in order to develop and live. They can be separated into primary consumers, those which feed directly on the producer level, such as deer or caterpillars, or secondary consumers, carnivores, feeding on the primary consumers. Beneath the producers are the decomposers, which include many bacteria, fungi and soil arthropods, that feed on dead and decaying materials from both the consumers and the producers. The organic matter synthesized by the trees is thus consumed by a series of levels, the trophic levels, and, with the aid of the decomposers, is eventually broken down and returned to the producers for re-use.

Unfortunately, the above details drastically oversimplify reality. It is obvious that not all organisms fit tightly within any of the above trophic categories. Many overlap, being partial herbivores and partial carnivores; but it does allow us to draw some general conclusions about the properties of the ecosystem. Not all of the material synthesized by the trees is passed on to the primary consumers and then on to the secondary consumers. Some will be lost in metabolic processes or as waste products such as faeces or urine, and many plants will escape being consumed. There is a loss of material and energy as we pass from the producers through the ascending scale of consumers and thus a decrease in the number of animals that can be supported. As a result we find a pyramidal structure of trophic levels, the total number of organisms in each trophic class decreasing as we ascend the trophic scale.

However, it is not the sheer number of organisms within each trophic category which is important but their impact, so we use the total weight of living material, called the biomass, to look at the relative balance of different trophic levels within an ecosystem. In a woodland dominated by oak and beech an acre of land is likely to contain 100 tonnes of woody plants, much of the weight lying on the ground; half a tonne of herbaceous plants; rather less than 1 kg of large mammals such as deer, about 2 kg of small mammals such as rodents, just under 0.5 kg of birds and half a ton of the larger invertebrate animals, including 225 kg of earthworms, 22 kg of spiders, 4 kg of beetles and 40 kg of slugs and snails. Also within the soil there are nearly 4 tonnes of bacteria and 143 kg of protozoa. From this list we can see that a huge tonnage of plant material supports a comparatively small number of consumers and a vast bulk of decomposers.

FLUX AND FLOW

Throughout the ecosystem there is a transfer, storage and dissipation of energy flowing through individual organisms, the network of the food web and the trophic levels. There is also a continual cycle of nutrients between the biotic (living) and abiotic (non-living) environments. Chemicals in flux include carbon, oxygen, hydrogen and nitrogen, and not only involves the solid or liquid dimensions, but also the gas phase, carbon dioxide being one of the prime requirements for photosynthesis. Because of this cycling the importance of the decomposers cannot be underrated: if they were absent all the useful organic material would soon be bound up in living tissue or trapped and quite unusable within dead tissue. A vast spectrum of decomposers works continuously on leaf litter, animal faeces and carrion and it is largely the unseen micro-organisms, the bacteria and fungi, which are responsible for the full decay of all the biotic waste, releasing the essential nutrients back to the producers for reuse.

The dominance and the actual role of any one species in the dynamics of the system shifts and alters. Some of the changes are short-term and cyclic, some are time-dependent, for example, the activity of different groups of animals exploiting the day and night. Kestrels *Falco tinnunculus* and Sparrowhawks *Accipiter nisus* are the principal predators during the day, and their roles are taken up at night by Tawny Owls *Strix aluco* and Barn

A Tawny Owl

Owls *Tyto alba* feeding on the same set of secondary consumers, voles and mice. Throughout the seasons plants too may be present or absent from the community as germination and re-emergence of different species occurs at different times. Flowering time and the pattern of domination of the community may show a cycle of change as well. Indeed, deciduous oak woodland is just at one end of such a change, in the sense that it is the final product of a succession of plant communities that starts with bare ground and moves through a range of seral changes before it reaches the mature stage.

HISTORY

In northern Europe the climatic climax plant community is currently Atlantic Forest. This is a mixed deciduous woodland which, since the beginning of the present interglacial period 10,000 years ago, has changed continually in its species composition. When the ice first retreated Birch

Betula spp., Scots Pine *Pinus sylvestris* and Aspen *Populus tremula* predominated. Later English Elm *Ulmus procera*, Wych Elm *Ulmus glabra*, Common Hazel *Corylus avellana* and Oak *Quercus* sp. joined the evergreen Holly *Ilex aquifolium*. Common Ash *Fraxinus excelsior* arrived 9,000 years ago along with Common Beech *Fagus sylvatica*, Field Maple *Acer campestre* and Hornbeam *Carpinus betulus*, but these species were much slower to spread. In fact, Common Ash only really became established with the demise of Common Lime *Tilia* × *europaea*, which was cleared by early farmers for feeding their livestock about 5,000 years ago. At this point Atlantic Forest or wildwood, as it was known, with all its diversity and dynamisms, was about to be changed irreversibly. Man had discovered agriculture and began felling and burning to provide space for his cattle. By Roman times crop farming was still only local in Britain but the Landnam method of cutting, burning, clearing, sowing, reaping and abandoning had become established, leaving many cleared areas nutritionally raped and on these the forest has never regrown.

Not all the trees were simply destroyed, however. About 4,000 years ago the techniques of pollarding (the cutting of trees 3–4 m above the ground, followed by a period of regrowth and then successive harvesting) and coppicing (the cutting of trees at ground level, followed by regrowth and then successive harvesting) were developed and trees such as beech, oak and hazel were yielding sustainable crops. Later iron was discovered; making clearances easier, creating a demand for fuel for smelting and a prosperity which led to a demand for more agriculture. By the time the Romans left and the Saxons arrived, half of the wildwood had been cleared and by the time the Domesday Book was compiled in 1086 only a sixth remained. In the centuries that followed, kilns required fuel to make bricks to build houses, and the nations of Europe were having fun at sea with their navies. More trees fell. At this stage some attempts were made to regulate the management of woodland but the wildwood had gone and Europe was now a place of open landscapes.

So what's left? In 1980 about seven per cent of Britain was wooded, much of it being large, sterile blocks of conifers planted on the uplands of Wales and Scotland. Since the end of the Second World War oak woodland has also suffered at the hands of encroaching Sycamore *Acer pseudoplatanus*, ash and birch, which have driven out the endemic species. The abandoning of many old coppices has led to a small increase in deciduous woodland in places, as the woods are allowed to mature, but overall the story is still one of sad decline.

UNION OF PRODUCERS

Today in Britain we have two species of oak, the Pedunculate or English Oak *Quercus robur* and the Sessile or Durmast Oak *Q. petraea*. The former is typical of woodland in central, south-eastern and most of southern England whilst the latter is commoner in the hill and mountain regions of the west. Joining these oaks are an array of other trees including: the Wych Elm, which is commoner in the west and north; the Common Ash, which forms pure woods on shallow limestone soil and likes wetter oak-woods; the Field Maple, which is common in southern English oak-woods; the Sycamore which is an introduced invader from southern continental Europe; the Hornbeam, which is only found in a restricted area of south-west England; and the Alder, which grows in wet depressions in oak-woods or forms pure woods on undrained soils. Other trees such as birches, Aspen, the poplars *Populus* spp., Wild Cherry *Prunus avium*, Bird Cherry *P. padus*, Crab Apple *Malus sylvestris*, Wild Service Tree and Holly are also found in association with oaks. Hazel is the commonest shrub of this woodland and typically grows by producing multiple stems at its base. Coppicing encouraged this and in some places pure hazel-woods are found. Hawthorn *Crataegus monogyna*, Blackthorn *Prunus spinosa* and the sallows *Salix* spp. are all also abundant. Oak-wood shrubs and Guelder Rose *Viburnum opulus*, Bramble *Rubus* sp., evergreen Ivy *Hedera helix* and Honeysuckle *Lonicera periclymenum* often form the lower shrub layer.

The composition of the field layer depends greatly on the type of soil the oak-wood is growing on. On lighter soils Bracken *Pteridium aquilinium* often dominates and with it Creeping Soft-grass *Holcus mollis* often grows, vegetating before the Bracken fronds are fully expanded and have formed a dense canopy. The Bluebell *Hyacinthoides non-scriptus* grows even earlier than the soft-grass, between February and May, and thus completes nearly all of its photosynthetic activity before the Bracken and oak canopies close and reduce the floor to darkness. It is interesting to note that the fine carpets of bluebell seen in spring only occur in British woods and are not seen at all on the continent. Wood Anemone *Anemone nemorosa* and Lesser Celandine *Ranunculus ficaria* are two other very common plants of early spring, along with Primrose *Primula vulgaris*, the more restricted Oxlip *P. elatior* and the Common Dog Violet *Viola riviniana*. Dog's Mercury *Mercurialis perennis* and Sanicle *Sanicula europaea* also flower early but unlike the others their leafy shoots continue to flourish on through the shady summer. Other oak-wood species include Wild Strawberry *Fragaria vesca*, Enchanters Nightshade *Circaea lutetiana*, Ground Ivy *Glechoma hederacea*, Burdock *Arctium minus*, Wood Sedge *Carex sylvatica*, Broad-leaved Willow-herb *Epilobium montanum*, Yellow Archangel *Lamiastrum galeobdolon*, Wood Sorrel *Oxalis acetosella*, Betony *Stachys officinalis* and the grasses *Brachypodium sylvaticum* and *Poa nemoralis*.

The ground layer generally has species of mosses like *Atrictium undulatum* and *Thurdium tarmariscunium*, with species of *Polytrichum* on more acid soils.

While in the oak-woods this vast and diverse array of shrubs and flowers flourishes in a succession of splendour throughout the season, the beech-wood's deep shade precludes all but a few species. The beech is a dominant and aggressive tree, suppressing all rivals and forming pure woods. These woodlands are now confined to southern and south-eastern England where they grow on the chalk, limestone and loamy soils of the escarpments and valley sides. Occasionally Ash, Whitebeam *Scorbus aria* and Wild Cherry are found as small strangled survivors in such woods, but generally only the evergreens such as Yew *Taxus baccata*, Holly and Box *Buxus sempervirens* thrive.

The field layer is also weak and generally Ivy, Dog's Mercury and Sanicle dominate while Green Hellebore *Helleborus viridis*, Columbine *Aquilegia vulgaris*, Common Solomon's Seal *Polygonatum multiflorum* and Sweet Woodruff *Galium odoratum* are much less common plants. Of special interest, however, are the helleborines *Epipactus* and *Cephalanthera* spp. and other orchids which flower in the deep shade. Mosses are absent from the ground layer since they cannot establish themselves in the thick leaf litter.

These producers, in all their combinations, diversity and spatial complexity, give rise to a monumental assemblage of consumers and decomposers. Mammals, birds, reptiles, amphibians, insects, crustaceans and fungi all inhabit woodlands in such a bewildering array that to try and summarize even one group would take the remainder of this book and reduce the subject to the superficial. Thus I will draw from the above groups a few key species, almost at random, and attempt to illustrate the woodland habitat using these and tiny facets of their complex life forms and lifestyles. What better way to start than on a sunny June day and a spectacle which you could commonly watch anywhere in the British Isles?

SPECKLED WOODS

By early summer the woodland's canopy of leaves has closed like a green velvet curtain over the lower layers of life. The interior of the wood becomes like a lonely old parish church – silent, musty, exclusive and freckled with patches of sunlight. Here and there the light strikes violently, like static lightning, turning the foliage into displays of smashed emerald. On the path ahead, some distance away you may notice some manic movement in such a spot. When you arrive all is apparently still, but, curious, you stand and watch.

Then the sunspot explodes. The puppeteer's gone berserk again. A pair of Speckled Wood butterflies *Pararge aegeria* engages in a deranged dance, flashing and flickering in a revelation of sunshine and violence. Butterflies fighting – sounds impossible, but the beauty of their form is overruled by their dynamic intentions. As usual it's down to Darwin and his fitness workout, because this pretty spectacle of sunbathed freneticism is in reality a bitter battle, with the winner's prize courtship. Somehow these less-than-paperweights are beating each other up! But what fun. The pair may be joined by as many as four or five individuals in a tumbling cohesion of gossamer. Up and down they go, twisting, turning, retreating and returning, at times they pack tightly and look like one mad rag, then they pulse apart only to coalesce again, like electrons around an atom's nucleus. Eventually there is fission and the demented display dissolves. The nucleus remains and when he settles the scene becomes slightly static, he only turns now and then on his sunspot, twitching his wings casually in anticipation or preparation. Not since Pizarro killed Atahualpa have men fought for the sun, for energy from ninety-three million miles away. These boys battle for minutes of sunshine on one day in one

LEFT **A Silver-washed Fritillary drinking at a woodland pool**
RIGHT **Beech woodland**

spot. Their mock fighting is a palatable pleasantness in comparison with other territorial behaviour. It is without doubt a beautiful ballet, but why does it happen?

Speckled Wood butterflies spend their nights roosting high up in the tree-tops. In the early morning, as the warmth of the sun reaches the foliage of the woodland canopy, the butterflies open their wings and orientate themselves parallel to the sun's rays to warm themselves up. Having reached a suitable temperature, they begin flying about. Gradually over the next hour or two the males descend to ground level where the sun has begun to cast pools of sunlight on the woodland floor. From then on, up until early evening these males can be found fluttering close to these sunny spots, their light providing sufficient warmth to enable the butterflies to remain active in the otherwise dark wood.

Individual males often spend the entire day in one sunspot. As the sun moves across the sky and the spot moves, they follow it, always keeping within the boundary of light. During the day they will move up to 50 metres in this way, following their sunspot's movement across the woodland floor. They perch on prominent vegetation in the sunspot, usually on a frond of bracken or on a bramble leaf and, using this as a base, fly out to inspect all passing objects. These bases, or the sunspots as a whole, form the territories which males will always compete for. Only sixty per cent of the males generally hold such territories while the remainder patrol the air space in the tree canopy. These aerial tramps occasionally fly down from the canopy and avidly take over any vacant sunspots. However, if the sunspot is already occupied then the 'intruder' is always driven back by the 'owner'. Experiments have shown that this is true even if the 'owner' has been in occupation for only a few seconds. Actual ownership is gained by physically landing on the sunspot – those which flutter near it but don't actually make contact can only regard themselves as intruders. Thus, the rule for settling the

contest is resident wins, intruder retreats, regardless of the condition of the resident male. Even tatty old boys with torn wings who were owners, did not lose to intruders who were young assailants in mint condition. The contests only escalate to the heights described earlier when two or more contestants all think that they are the resident. The reason why intruders accept defeat so graciously and without a serious fight may be that defence of a sunspot is risky, in terms of wasted time and energy, because of the risk of crippling physical injuries, such as wing damage during one of the exciting spiral flights, and because the intruder and the owner are equally able to fight for the sunspot since there is no benefit to the owner in learning the territory's characteristics. These are anyway continually changing as the sunspot moves throughout the day.

Violent affrays occur more frequently at the beginning of the season, and when the weather is bad, because the lower temperature makes the sunny spots more limited and therefore more valuable to the males. Their value, as you might have imagined, is due to their status as mating-rendezvous sites.

In order to mate, if you're a butterfly, you have to be hot: so males fight for the right to sit in front of the fire! If you watch a male long enough, especially in the morning, you may witness this mating. When a female enters his solarium he will fly after her, eventually chasing her to the ground, where a courtship dance ensues. This consists of a series of jerky wing movements after which the male bends his abdomen sideways to initiate copulation. It is all over in less than a minute and he immediately tears off back to his old sunspot. But what if one of the tree-top marauders has since put his six feet down and claimed his resident status? Surely having jetted his genes into the next population the mated beau should be content. But no, nature's impetuous greed impels him to fight for more, and occasionally he may regain his status as owner after a short tussle. Once again

A Speckled Wood

he can bask in the energy from our yellow star and try to keep pace with the movement of the planet, following its effects without knowing the cause.

OTHER WOODLAND BUTTERFLIES

The resplendent Purple Emperor butterfly *Apatura iris* can be a most frustrating insect, spending most of its time careering around the tops of large oak trees in a powerful, gliding flight. To see them at close range is a rare event, and only really possible if they have descended to the woodland floor to feed by sipping at rotting carrion, dung or woodland puddles.

The caterpillar, which has a slug-like appearance, feeds on sallow leaves. It is a soft, light green, speckled with white dots, and is pointed at both ends; the head end is adorned with two greenish-blue horns knobbed with red. Although ostentatious this colouration makes it very difficult to see on the sallow leaves. In November it further camouflages itself when it moves to the fork of a sallow branch and changes its

colour to a dingy greeny-brown, at the same time aligning itself with the grain of the wood. The following June the larva transforms into a leaf-like chrysalis which gives rise to the adult in mid-July.

Unfortunately these butterflies are uncommon, and on many visits to a local wood where they are reputed to exist I have spent more time watching the less salubrious activities of collectors than the habits of this extraordinary insect. Surely it is time that butterfly-collecting was made illegal, like the similarly selfish and outdated pursuit of egg-collecting, or do we have to wait until it's too late? On the continent, however, this species can be quite common in places and the similar, yet smaller, Lesser Purple Emperor *Apatura ilia* can also be found.

Another striking woodland butterfly is the White Admiral *Limenitis camilla* which has black upper-wings with white transverse bands. These serve to disrupt the outline of the wing and, in the dappled light of the woodland clearings, individuals seem to vanish before your eyes. In flight it has an elegant gliding and fluttering motion, and when it alights, usually on bramble and honeysuckle bloom, it does so with its wings wide open. Bramble clumps are also the favourite flitting grounds of the Silver-washed Fritillary *Argynnis paphia* which appears in high summer. Its powerful fluttering and gliding flight distinguishes it from the much rarer Heath *Mellicta athalia* and High Brown *Fabriciana adippe* Fritillaries and from the much smaller Pearl-bordered *Clossiana euphrosyne* and Small Pearl-bordered *C. selene* Fritillaries which appear much earlier. Although violet is the larval food-plant the female Silver-washed Fritillaries actually lay their eggs in the crevices in the bark of a nearby tree-trunk. The caterpillars hatch in August and devour their egg-shell casing. Then, without eating anything else, they winter on the tree until March, when they descend up to a metre to the ground in search of their food-plant. The larvae then gorge themselves on violets until they pupate in June, the horned chrysalis hanging beneath the underside of a violet leaf until mid-July when the adult emerges.

Another group of butterflies which inhabits the woodlands is the hairstreaks, but if anything these are more difficult to observe than the fritillaries, since when they do rest it is generally high in the canopy. The commonest of these, and most widely distributed, is the Purple Hairstreak *Quercusia quercus*, which can usually be seen dancing in a mad fluttering flight around the uppermost branches of their favourite oak trees. The Brown Hairstreak *Thecla betulae* frequents Blackthorn thickets and can be seen feeding on Bramble blossom, while the Black Hairstreak *Strymonidia pruni*, one of our rarest indigenous butterflies, can be seen around the former. The White-letter Hairstreak *Strymonidia w-album*, easily distinguished from relatives by the W pattern on the undersides of its wings, is dependent on Wych or Common Elm for its food-plant,

and so in recent years has decreased as the elms have succumbed to the ravages of Dutch elm disease. Other woodland butterflies include: the Wood White *Leptidea sinapis*, a rather locally distributed, delicate and weakly-flying insect which only appears for a short time, which may be further curtailed by bad, windy weather; the Large Tortoiseshell *Nymphalis polychloros* which is now rare, if not extinct over much of the British Isles; and the Duke of Burgundy Fritillary *Hamearis lucina* which is a local species in Britain but quite widespread on the continent.

Once you have been snagged by brambles, trodden in dung, got twigs in your eye and wet feet to identify your long-pursued fritillary or hairstreak, look at it more superficially, as a child might. It will see you through two large compound eyes, each formed from many minute facets or ommatidia. These will not form thousands of little pictures of you, but one single composite image within its tiny brain. These eyes not only perceive your towering movement but also basically detect light and dark as well as colour, and may be able to see over a much greater range of the spectrum than we can. Pause to look at its unwieldy antennae projecting in a ridiculous fashion from the butterfly's brow, and covered in millions of microscopic scent organs for dissecting every smell in the insect's surroundings. Look at this insect's mouthparts, coiled like a ridged watch-spring under the eyes. This proboscis pulses between the enlarged palps on the underside of the head when feeding and may probe between the scales on the wing as if preening like a bird. Look at its bulbous, hairy body, ventilated not by conventional lungs but by fibrous respiratory tubules called trachea, which run throughout the body and open to small holes called spiracles on the sides of the abdomen. Lastly, look at the beautiful but stupid wings. Slight slivers of veined tissue, full of living blood pumping through crazy-coloured canals which all return to the base; the base where these impossible structures are strapped to a flight mechanism which has been actively propelling this type of insect for 270 million years. A simply designed box, with muscles pulling to and fro, manipulates the wings in unison and has the ability for instantaneous flight and instantaneous stopping, enabling remarkable acceleration and deceleration, exerting tremendous forces on the tiny thorax. And yet by the laws of physics, with their low aspect ratios and high induced drag, basically dreadful aerodynamics, these insects are not capable of flight by normal aerofoil action. Instead they use a clap–fling mechanism, whereby at the end of each downstroke a swirling vortex of air is shed beneath the butterfly. It is the force needed to create this whirling mass of air which sustains the insect's flight, an upward reaction from the vortex rings as they are flung downwards. It really doesn't matter which butterfly it is, or how rare it is, or how mad its life-style is. Just its basic physical form is amazing enough.

ORCHIDS AND HELLEBORINES

The name of the Greater Butterfly Orchid *Platanthera chlorantha* is derived from the shape of its flowers and not from its flight capabilities! These flowers appear predominantly in June, are white tinged with green, and are studded with two bright yellow capsules of pollen. Up to twenty-five may occur on a stem, set on their long, slightly S-shaped ovaries, giving the whole spike a broad appearance. Each is embellished with a very long tubicular spur, which projects out behind the flower and round the other side of the spike, curving downwards in a gentle semi-circle. The entrance to this spur is wide and clearly visible at the throat of the flower and it is here that moths are drawn by the strong, sweet scent emitted at night. Only these insects have long enough tongues to reach the nectar this holds, but as they thrust their heads into the flower sticky pads, called viscidia, are tightly glued to their eyes. These pads are at the base of a stalked structure which holds the pollen

The Great Butterfly Orchid

capsules or pollenia. When the insect leaves this flower, taking the whole structure with it, the stalks swivel forwards so that the next flower visited has the pollenia pushed on to its stigma, and cross-pollination is effected. The Greater Butterfly Orchid grows in shaded areas with a mossy humus for its roots which, like those of many orchids, are entwined with a fungus partner and run out through the soil from two egg-shaped tubers. Such a symbiotic relationship means that even in the deep shade, where these plants can gather little energy from the sun, they can acquire all they need from their fungal partners' activities in the rotting humus. These mycorrhizal fungi belong predominantly to the genus *Rhizoctonia*. They initially attack the germinating orchid parasitically, but this intrusion is rebuffed and in turn they are digested by the cells of the orchid. From then on this love–hate nutritional seesawing begins to fluctuate, the dominance of each partner varying with seasons. In the light of spring and summer the orchid is dominant, but in autumn and winter, when the activity of the plant's physiological processes are at their lowest level, the fungus prevails in the symbiotic relationship. In many species of orchid a mycorrhizal relationship is only really important for germination and those which later grow large tubers tend to become independent of their fungal partner. Species, including many helleborines, with extensive, shallow rooting systems in the surface humus are usually dependent on the fungus throughout their life.

Europe has fifteen species of helleborine, many of which, in the northern parts of their range, are plants of wooded areas. These include the Narrow-leaved Helleborine *Cephalanthera longifolia*, which takes eight years to mature; the White Helleborine *Cephalanthera damasonium* whose flowers never open properly in Britain; the commonest and widespread Broad-leaved Helleborine *Epipactis helleborine*, which can be readily discovered in most older woodlands; the Violet Helleborine *E. purpurata* which may grow in attractive clumps of up to twenty spikes; the Narrow-lipped Helleborine *E. leptochila*, first described in Britain in 1919 and an exceptionally efficient self-pollinator; and the Pendulous or Green-flowered Helleborine *E. phyllanthes*, a small and delicate cousin of the rest of the helleborines in which self-fertilization occurs within the unopened flower. But by far the most exciting of our woodland helleborines is the Red Helleborine *C. rubra* and in July of 1986 I set out to see this extraordinary plant.

It had just rained and a clammy stillness hung under the beeches. A Great Spotted Woodpecker rapped about a mile away and my boots stuck on the sticky chalk path which twisted out of the wood between the ruins of Ramsons and a sea of Dog's Mercury. I felt like a pilgrim with an incurable disease trekking for a cure but it was a miracle I was looking for.

The Red Helleborine was probably never common in Britain, certainly not since the Bronze and Iron Age clearances. It is an incredible specialist and, because of its mad lifestyle, in England it has committed ecological suicide. The flowering of this plant is governed by incident light levels deep in beech woodland. Its precise requirements are unknown, but if it has too much light it won't thrive, and if it is too dark it won't flower. Consequently it has developed the ability to live as an underground rhizome which occasionally produces leaves and can survive for up to fifteen years without flowering, all this time being dependent on its fungus partner for nutrition. When it does flower, pollination may be effected by small bees or hover-flies, or it is more likely to be self-pollinating at the bud stage. Let's face it, this semi-celibate hermaphrodite is a sexual flop and this is partly why it is so rare. Certainly its extreme beauty meant that it was formerly picked. I expect that pasty-faced little sixteenth-century woodcutters' daughters brought bunches back to their smoky hovels to enrich their plagued and oppressed lives with its beauty.

Today, the Red Helleborine is said to grow at only two or three locations in southern England. I was at a fourth after thieving some conversational fragments overheard in the company of my orchidophile elders. All I wanted was to see one of these plants in flower.

The path reached a stile submerged in Cow Parsley on the edge of the wood and a pile of beer cans reminded me I was in 1986 and not 1586. Over the stile it dissolved into a rich, dark, decaying soil and weaving through a quilted carpet of green and brown I soon found some expired spikes of Bird's-nest Orchids *Neottia nidus-avis*, those anaemic yellowy-brown cousins of the helleborines, who have given up any chance of using light and have become entirely saphrophytic on their fungus partners. I could have found these within a quarter of an hour from home, so I was hardly satiated. I made my way through the wood, staring dizzily at the carpet of leaves. The error that just one false step could make made me intensely cautious over every footfall. Thus walking like a drunk on broken glass I literally, or rather not literally, stumbled over it. Standing about five metres from a smallish beech with a few bits of grass, yet definitely alone and aloof was that elixir of England that I'd just about kill for. What an extrovert! Those flowers were the richest blemish on the woodland palette, a dramatic mistake in this dirge of green. I went down on my knees in front of it. I wanted to get inside those flowers, I wanted my whole world to be a rich, reddish-purple-pink-magenta-violet. The zig-zaggy stem was about 25 cm high and had spear-shaped, limp, dark green leaves from top to bottom. There were five flowers, somewhat like freesias, the upper part being

flattish and the lower ship-shaped, giving it a bell-like appearance. Inside, a number of finely haired, orange ridges led you into the core, where a sticky, twisted stigma was covered in the neatest down imaginable. It was so fragile. It would have died of thirst compressed by blotting paper in a flower press. I could have made its roots scream by potting it in the illuminated insanity of my greenhouse. But it was a pure, untainted, unpolluted and unchanged symbol and the thought of this beautiful plant's destruction was beyond my possible comprehension. Surely any and every living person could admire and understand this badge of beauty. I photographed it from every angle for over an hour, all the while on a jittery edge because of my trespass and insane jealousy, feeling like a naughty schoolboy looking at his first pornographic magazine.

Trapped in the shade of a beech wood, the saprophytic Birds'-nest Orchid

The cold bites your toes and the inky trees whisper gently as they disappear into the sky. They look like black cracks in the celestial bowl, a dark, dark blue bowl which is studded with billions of stars spread out in the most beautiful of all patterns, the pattern made by millions of little fragments of light which twinkled in the eyes of the Jurassic giants, the Pleistocene mammals, Iron Age man, and now still burn as jewels of foreverness.

WOODLAND WADER

It's March and I am lying on my back in the crispy decay of last year's leaves. Just what my mother said I shouldn't do. I am waiting for a bird, and I know my wait won't be long. He's very predictable, and unusual, because the Woodcock *Scolopax rusticola* is a wader who probes woodland streams rather than any estuary mud.

I hear him long before I see him. 'Tsiwick . . . Tsiwick . . . orrrt-orrrt', then out of the black-blueness, over the trees, he appears in Orion, blots out Rigel, then Betelgeuse, bends slightly in his otherwise straight flight and passes through Gemini on his broad wings. By Ursa Major he is overhead and his long prospecting beak is clearly visible. 'Tsiwick . . . Tsiwick . . . orrrt-orrrt', past Bootes the herdsman, 'Tsiwick . . . Tsiwick . . . orrrt-orrrt', a million light years across the night sky and then he vanishes into the stars of another hemisphere out over the woods. Still, I hear, 'Tsiwick . . . Tsiwick . . . orrrt-orrrt,' in fact within a quarter of an hour our astronomer is back, bill down, twisking and croaking overhead in his roding display flight.

Although this species is a wader and superficially similar to the Snipe *Gallinago gallinago* it does not habitually wade or swim. It is a ground-loving bird which likes dry, warm resting places accompanied by clear open ground of the type found in mature woodlands, particularly of oak and birch. Up until the 1970s very little was

LEFT **Tawny Owl**
RIGHT **Inky trees**

known of this curious creature, which is somewhat surprising since men have successfully shot at it for centuries. Then a friend of mine, Graham Hirons, had a few good ideas. . . .

Being almost wholly nocturnal and favouring thicker parts of woodlands, the problem had always been spotting and observing the Woodcock. Graham, however, learnt that Basque hunters used to throw their hats up under roding males in order to lure them down into nets and thus into their cooking pots. When this method failed to give results, perhaps British Woodcocks were too discerning to succumb to Graham's array of headpieces, he discovered 'Spiteful', a friend's tawny bantam. Seated in a hide on the edge of a clearing and surrounded by a cage of invisible mist nets, Graham waited for a roding bird to fly overhead before throwing Spiteful into her arena. Immediately amorous male woodcock were gripped with a passion for Spiteful and up to three a night would plummet headlong into the nets. This is where the science begins, because previously it was thought that a single male would rode a set path each night, delineating his territory. Now up to three could be called down from one such path.

With the help of his chicken, Graham went on to discover that this form of self-advertising display flight is in fact used by a succession of males between March and July to find females who observe the aerobatics from the ground. These females first choose a nesting area in the woods, which they occupy for about a week prior to finding a mate. Then they move to a clearing at dusk to listen to the roding males, which they can identify individually by their calls. Those males which rode for the longest time each night, up to 40 minutes, are most successful in finding mates. As it gets darker their slow, deliberate wing-beats guide the birds lower and lower over the clearings which are focal points for woodcock activity. These longer roders are generally older birds and eventually, when a female has made her choice, she flies up

below her intended mate and he swoops down giving a churring call before they come to rest. Occasionally this feminine action excites the attention of more than one male and Graham once saw seven males chasing one female off into the darkness. Normally, however, the chosen male is led back to the nesting area where courtship takes place. This consists of the birds turning in circles, raising tails, tapping bills and fluttering round with half-open wings. The climax occurs when the pair jump about excitedly before copulation. The hen then chooses her exact nest site, usually concealed by brambles close to the base of a tree. During this period, usually three or four days, the male is always in attendance, ensuring that the female resists the attentions of any other suitors. As soon as she has laid her four eggs, however, he deserts her to return to roding. The most successful males can father four broods a year, while their abandoned mates incubate their eggs for all but half an hour a day when they sneak off to feed.

The Woodcock's food is predominantly animal material, particularly earthworms and the larvae of various insects, although some plant food may be taken from frozen ground or from under snow. The bird slowly picks the food from the ground and may be seen turning over matted clumps of leaves with its bill, sometimes walking rapidly to and fro, stabbing deliberately at the ground in a typical wader fashion. Once prey is detected, using the supersensitive bill tip, the bill is stabbed in to its full length, using several very rapid thrusting movements. When a worm is encountered it is seized and slowly extracted with the aid of a spiny tongue. If the worm is large and deep this process may prove very difficult and the beak is twisted from side to side, the bird's wings flapping madly as it tries to prise it from the damp soil. All of this behaviour Graham and other scientists managed to observe because they had fitted radio transmitters to the Woodcock. This enabled them to locate the birds without disturbing them, both in the day and at night. The amateur observer, however, has to be content to watch the roding flights which can be seen throughout the British Isles at dusk.

THE WOODLAND DRUMMERS
In Britain only three species of woodpecker are resident, the Green, the Great Spotted and the Lesser Spotted Woodpecker. In Europe, however, these are joined by the Grey-headed Woodpecker *Picus canus*, the Syrian Woodpecker *Dendrocopus syriacus*, the Middle Spotted Woodpecker *D. medius*, the White-backed Woodpecker *D. leucotos*, the Three-toed Woodpecker *Picoides tridactylus*, and the Wryneck *Jynx torquilla*, which is not strictly a woodpecker but shares their feeding habits. With such a bevy of chisel-billed birds, climbing tree-trunks to search out their invertebrate prey, we can well ask how such a collection of similar species can co-exist in the one deciduous woodland habitat?

Each organism within a community occupies a niche, and this niche is described as a 'multidimensional hypervolume defined by the sum of all the interactions of that organism and its biotic and abiotic environment'. What this bulky and scientific bonanza means is that the organism's role includes more than just its address (where it is) and its profession (what it does) within the community, because the various relationships it has with other organisms around it and the role it plays in the operation of the community as a whole are also involved. Its population dynamics, feeding relationships and competitive interactions form its niche which is the ecological functioning of that organism within the whole woodland ecosystem. If within a group of similar species, such as the woodpeckers, niches overlap with other niches on any of the parameters such as their address or profession, competition develops, and the aim of any individual and species is to reduce this competition by attempting to separate their niches. This will lead to a strong tendency

for each species to specialize, indeed to become a separate species, and then to utilize one particular portion of the resource not utilized by the other competing species. In reality there are, of course, many methods to achieve this aim. If we consider feeding, different woodpecker species may feed at different times, or in different places, or on slightly different prey, on different trees at different heights or different stages of decomposition. In the case of these birds it is likely that most of these parameters will be exploited since, with so many species attempting to occupy this particular environment, the resource is likely to be divided up between them in such a way that nearly all of its available attributes are fully utilized in order to keep competition to an absolute minimum. But enough of the scientific principles. In real terms how do all these woodpeckers co-exist in our woodlands?

The Green Woodpecker is the most specialized of all of the species, but despite its large size it has the weakest bill. Consequently, it is unable to chisel wood and spends nearly all of its time foraging on the ground for ants and their pupae. These it finds by patrolling woodland rides and clearings, and once a nest is located it may be visited two or three times before it is exhausted. Green Woodpeckers, unlike the following species, have smooth, sticky tongues which can stretch up to 10 cm in length.

The slightly smaller Grey-headed Woodpecker is a species midway between the Green and the *Dendrocopos* species. It too likes ants, but it also spends some of its feeding time in the trees. The Greater Spotted Woodpecker does not feed from the ground at all. It chisels for food in the canopy in the top of the tree and has a varied diet, mainly of insects, but also including birds' eggs and winter seeds. The Syrian Woodpecker avoids competition with these species by taking prey from less deeply in thicker branches. The less energetic Three-toed Woodpecker isolates itself by feeding lower down on the main branches of the trees where it picks insects off the bark.

The Middle Spotted and White-backed Woodpeckers avoid competition with the above by foraging exclusively on dead trees. To prevent competition between themselves, the White-backed only exploits stumps and fallen timber, where it digs very deep for beetle larvae, etc. Lastly, the tiny Lesser Spotted Woodpecker hunts high in the crowns of trees amongst the thin twigs, where it is adept at snatching food from under leaves.

Having successfully spaced themselves out over the tree-gleaning resource, the solution of the problem of competition is not over for these species. In most of the *Dendrocopos* group, males and females forage differently. The males have larger bills and specialize in the lower part of the species' feeding niche whilst the lighter females forage higher in the trees on the smaller trunks, branches and twigs. Thus these woodpeckers have sufficiently spaced their niches to enable them to co-exist, and in some parts of Europe six or seven of the species can be found in the same woodland.

THE CATCHERS OF FLIES

In Britain three species of leaf warblers are found, the Wood Warbler *Phylloscopus sibilatrix*, the Willow Warbler *P. trochilus* and the Chiffchaff *P. collybita*. They are small, greenish-brown, lightly built birds, having a pale stripe above the eye and yellowish-green underparts. They flit about high in the tree canopy, feeding on insects with their delicate bills. In European woodlands they are joined by Arctic Warblers *P. borealis*, Greenish Warblers *P. trochiloides*, Bonelli's Warblers *P. bonelli*, and Yellow-browed Warblers *P. inornatus*. Initially all these species may be hard to separate in the field, but just like the woodpeckers they too have to space their niches out to enable them to co-exist, and so are in fact very different.

The Chiffchaff is the earliest of our spring migrants to return, arriving in early March to join some of its fellows which may have over-wintered in southern England. It requires bushy undergrowth to hide its nest and tall trees as song posts to overlook its feeding sites. The Willow Warbler will thrive in almost any wooded or open bushy area, and is a bird with an altogether cleaner appearance than the rather dingy Chiffchaff. It has a stronger eye-stripe and usually paler pinkish legs, although these may be difficult to see as it darts jerkily through the spangled canopy snatching tiny unseen insects.

The Wood Warbler is the most brightly coloured, having yellowish-green upper parts and a glowing sulphur-yellow throat and breast. This species is the last of the three to arrive and is not seen before mid-April when it becomes easily distinguishable by its marvellous song. This far-carrying trill, delivered from high in the roof of the forest, builds up to a crescendo of notes which reduces the whole bird to a quivering ball of feathered excitement. It filters down to the floor to your ricked neck and straining eyes, and just when you find the songster, it vanishes.

Wood Warblers are much more particular about their habitat, since they prefer mature beech and oak woodland, with little or no undergrowth, and are unfortunately the least common of the trio. Despite their highly arboreal nature all these species are ground-nesting. The females make compact, domed, almost spherical nests from leaves, grass, stalks and moss, and these are generally well hidden among low-growing plants and bushes.

At the end of summer these 10-gram birds and their numerous young have the prospect of a flight to their winter quarters in Africa. Thus they engage in an agile frenzy of feeding activity, nipping about in the tangle of sunlit leaves, hopping to and fro to pick up tiny insects, and zipping insanely from canopy to canopy snatching at flies, midges and moths.

The habit of intercepting insects in flight has, however, been more precisely perfected by another group of birds, the fly-

A clearing in an ancient beech woodland

catchers *Muscicapidae*. In Britain only two of Europe's four species are found. The Pied Flycatcher *Ficedula hypoleuca* is only really common in the western oakwoods of Wales. Its Spotted namesake *Muscicapa striata* can be seen performing its athletic feeding behaviour from April onwards, in most British woodland. Although not so strikingly coloured as the bold Pied, being a fawn brown and having an erectile spotted crest, they are nevertheless fascinating to watch.

When their aerial prey is scarce they are forced to move around the canopy in search of other prey, but here they are inept and clumsy, and hopping about in the twigs and branches their short, thin legs soon tire of this activity. Adults can only feed the young efficiently on large prey, and this may explain why the species is one of the last of the migrants to arrive in Europe, delaying their breeding season until warm weather is more likely to ensure the abundance of large flying insects. On arrival the birds quickly establish and maintain a defended territory, and within this use six to ten favourite feeding

perches to gather most of their food. Like all sit-and-wait predators, flycatchers expend a considerable amount of energy in the pursuit of prey, and so this hunting strategy has favoured the development of physical adaptations enabling them to deal with large prey items, such as large heads and bills. This makes their sallying flights more profitable per item. In fact by looking at their pattern of foraging in terms of which perch and how long each perch is used before it is given up, scientists have been able to discover that flycatchers switch between different foraging strategies and select prey so as to maximize their energy intake all the time. Changes in the diet were influenced by the density of the preferred aerial prey, and not that of the alternative prey hiding in the canopy. They can also recognize wasps and bees, and remove their stings before swallowing them. They also actually select different prey items when providing for their own and for their nestlings' diet in terms of nutrient and energy parameters. Thus these flycatcher gourmets individually snatch dishes from the dung-, house-

33

and hoverflies on offer while spending exactly the right amount of time perched in the best restaurant and the right amount of energy feeding there in order to optimize their airborne adventures.

AVIAN PREDATORS

In the field Sparrowhawks can be remarkably difficult to see. In flight they show pronounced countershading, with a dark bluey-grey upper surface and a pale black-barred underside. This dark–light pattern helps to break up their profile, the lighter underside being less obvious against the sky and the dark upper parts less visible against the ground. Like all woodland raptors they have short wings and a long tail and like many of them show horizontal barring on their underside, which also helps to break up the outline when the bird is perched amongst twigs and branches. The behaviour of Sparrowhawks also makes them difficult to observe because, except during their aerial displays in spring, they rarely show themselves, spending most of their time in deep cover. When they are in the open they usually fly close to the ground, taking advantage of any slight contour or irregularity in the terrain to keep themselves hidden. Flight consists of a brief series of rapid flaps, alternating with long glides, and because the bird is more noticeable when flapping, a surprise attack on prey is made with the final approach being in a long glide. When engaged in this *coup de grâce* the body is so slim and the wings so still and razor-thin that the front profile is almost invisible until the bird flicks out its extraordinarily long legs to quickly grab and pierce the flesh of its victim. Their feet are remarkably well developed for grasping their prey. The three front toes differ greatly in structure; the centre toe is long enough to extend the reach considerably and has a fleshy protuberance, on to which the razor-sharp claw can be closed to form a pincer; the opposed rear and outer toes are large and powerful, and are responsible for the holding, and in many cases the

killing, of the victim once it is caught, whilst the heavy inside claw of each foot is used to clamp the prey on the perch while it is plucked and torn apart by the feeding bird.

The Sparrowhawk's diet is entirely avian, the smaller male concentrating on smaller species and the female on larger prey up to the size of a Woodpigeon *Columba palumbus*. The most important prey species are song birds, such as the Chaffinch *Fringilla coelebs*, Song Thrush *Turdus philomelos*, Blackbird *Turdus merula*, Robin *Erithacus rubecula*, Starling *Sturnus vulgaris* and Meadow Pipit *Anthus pratensis*. Woodpigeons, Redwings *T. iliacus*, Fieldfares *T. pilaris*, Blue Tits *Parus caeruleus* and Great Tits *P. major* are also important at some time of year, and in some places Sparrowhawks probably account for more than half the total mortality in some of their prey species, and may take up to one-third of all the young tits fledged in any year. Like many raptors, they show a conspicuous size difference or dimorphism between the males and the females. There is a complex of reasons for this – the male, being the food provider, favours smallness and minimal body reserves; the female, needing a food storage capacity in order to breed, favours largeness for maximum reserves – but the size difference in fact influences most aspects of their lives. The males operate on a narrow safety margin and can starve within two or three days, while the females can last for four to six days without food. The female's increased size, however, is at the expense of agility and she is forced to take less manoeuvrable prey, including larger birds, together with more mammals and carrion, than the male. She is also less able to catch airborne prey in enclosed situations and thus hunts more in the open. All in all, size dimorphism gives the Sparrowhawk sexes a difference in diet and habitat choice which is greater than between many pairs of related species.

In most animals it is assumed that males invest less in reproduction because they produce an unlimited supply of tiny

Fiery-eyed and ferocious; a Goshawk

sperms and could in theory fertilize vast numbers of females, while these females have their capacity reduced since they need to produce large eggs and then rear the young. For this reason it is argued males should compete most heavily for females since these are the main resource necessary for breeding, and thus this fighting should lead to the development of secondary sexual characteristics such as larger body size, strength and fighting ability in the males. In the Sparrowhawk it is the other way round; almost the entire reproductive performance of the pair depends on the male. Whether the female will lay eggs at all, when she will lay, the clutch size, and the survival prospects of the young all depend on his foraging success. In contrast to most other animals therefore it is the male Sparrowhawk which invests most heavily in reproduction and upon him that the success of the pair largely depends. The reason for the female's larger size is not only so that she can hold larger food reserves during lean spells in the breeding season, but also so that she can be assured of securing the attention of the prime males by having physical superiority over the other females. Males will only normally pair with females in good condition, because only these can defend the nesting site against other females. Sparrowhawks of both sexes somehow also manage to select their mates to some extent by their age, since young birds are very infrequently found paired with adults that are older than them.

In many parts of Britain the Sparrowhawk is at the top of the avian food web; it is the principal predator which is preyed on by none – except man. Recently, however, its larger cousin the formidable Goshawk *Accipiter gentilis* has begun to breed here, as it does over much of Europe, and occasionally this species supplements its diet with the odd Sparrowhawk. Goshawks are large and very powerful, armed with muscular wings and legs, and heads studded with yellow-and-orange eyes which burn in a savage rage. To think of these out there, in our woods, flying about, killing, is awesome. To see them is even more difficult, since they are even more elusive than those devilishly sharp woodland weapons – the Sparrowhawks.

35

There was a table set out under a tree in front of the house, and the March Hare and the Hatter were having tea at it: a Dormouse was sitting between them, fast asleep, and the other two were using it as a cushion, resting their elbows on it, and talking over its head. 'Very uncomfortable for the Dormouse,' thought Alice; 'only, as it's asleep, I suppose it doesn't mind.'

Eventually, after some pretty dozy story-telling at the Mad Hatter's tea party, Lewis Carroll has the dormouse crammed into the teapot by the remaining participants. The unfortunate character was in fact a Common Dormouse *Muscardinus avellanarius* whose reputation for inactivity has given rise to a variety of local names: chestle-crumb, derry-mouse, dory-mouse, and dozing-mouse or even more blatantly the sleep mouse. All refer to this drowsy character in Alice's Adventures in Wonderland. Despite this lethargic nature they are a rather stupidly attractive animal of the cuddly genre. The tail and dense fur on the upper parts are a rich sandy-brown with a fine sprinkling of darker hairs, the eyes are large, prominent and black in colour, while the small rounded ears show clearly above the fur and it has extraordinarily long whiskers which measure up to 3 cm in length. The front feet are turned out laterally, almost at right angles to the body, so that the mouse finds it easier to climb twigs and branches using well-developed pads which assist in grasping and climbing. This adaptation is especially helpful because the animal seems to spend a lot of its time high in the thinner twigs of hazel, and when this tree was more frequently coppiced dormice must have been a lot more common than they are today. Indeed a recent Mammal Society survey has revealed a considerable decline since the beginning of the century and now these animals are most common in the south-west of England.

LEFT **The drowsy dormouse**
RIGHT **State of decay**

37

Finding dormice can be difficult because they can be incredibly unobtrusive. Stripped Honeysuckle can be a good indicator of the species's presence, because dormice are prolific nest-builders and most nests are comprised solely of this material. There are three types of nest: bulky summer breeding nests, which are usually above ground, rather smaller versions which are fashioned by the independent young of that summer, and winter nests in which individuals hibernate. Winter nests may be in a hollow tree, a hole under the ground, or amongst a thick carpet of leaves caught around the lower part of a tree-stump and may be spread around the dormouse's range, depending on the availability of sites. In mid-summer they often use more than one nest, and when the weather is colder up to five dormice may huddle together in one of these untidy balls. In the past the nocturnal habits of the dormouse rendered this species's behaviour almost unknown to science, rather like that of the Woodcock. Recently, however, scientists have tracked adult dormice using tiny radio transmitters fitted around the animals' short necks. These enabled them to follow the dormice at night for a period of ten days, before the lifetime of the transmitters' tiny batteries expired.

It now transpires that the preferred habitat is one with a thick species-rich shrub layer, through which dormice move about easily and very rapidly, often leaping gaps of 30 cm or more. Here they spend their time feeding in trees and shrubs, rarely venturing down to ground level. Because they can use their habitat in this more three-dimensional way their ground ranges are much smaller than that of the ground-living Wood Mice *Apodemus sylvaticus* and Bank Voles *Clethrionomys glareolus*. Interestingly, the actual three-dimensional area required to support ten dormice will support seventy Bank Voles and seventy Wood Mice. The scientists also discovered that during May dormice feed almost entirely in the tree canopy, and may spend several hours at a time in an oak tree feeding on catkins and insects. In June they make a greater use of the shrub layer where they search for aphids, Honeysuckle leaves and caterpillars and in July activity is concentrated in the canopy of ash trees where they slit open as many as three ash seeds in a minute. Later hazelnuts, acorns, Honeysuckle berries and other fruits become increasingly abundant, and the animals spend more time foraging in the shrub layer, storing fat for the approaching winter. Then, like bats, squirrels and hedgehogs, dormice avoid our cold and wet winter climate by entering a torpid state, reducing their metabolic rate to use less fat reserves. Not only mammals use this method of avoiding winter. Tucked in a crevice inside an ivy-covered hole, high on the lee side of an old oak tree, several queen Hornets *Vespa crabro* are hibernating.

HORNETS

To see a Hornet today is a treat. They are a richer ochre than the Common Wasp *Vespula vulgaris* and appear to fly slower and therefore stay in vision longer. They can appear much less frenzied, because of their less wavering flight and general disinterest in humans and, coupled with their lower density, this makes them a safer bet if you want to avoid minor insect sting injuries. If you were an insect, however, these blitzkrieg-big-brothers of wasps are decidedly dangerous.

In spring the queens emerge and disperse before they begin to build their embryo nests. Several loads of wood pulp are applied to the under surface of a hollow in a tree, often elm or oak, to form a sheet of paper before a spindle-like pillar is constructed downwards. When the spindle has been extended to about 12 mm in length, the next few loads of pulp are used to form the cup-like bases of the first two cells. When these have been initiated the queen begins to construct the envelope

RIGHT **The limbs of a tangled oak**

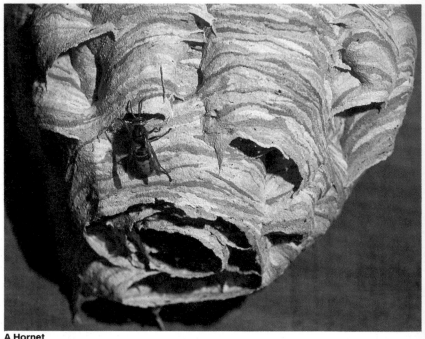

A Hornet

and umbrella-like structure which eventually surrounds the cells and provides some protection and insulation for the future brood. The ideal shape for a cell would be a cylinder, since this would be the best fit for the larval and pupal bodies. To save space, cylinders have to be packed in staggered rows so any three contiguous cells form an equilateral triangle, rather than a square. To save material each should share walls with its neighbours, and since each circle has six neighbours this means changing from a cylindrical to a hexagonal shape. This eliminates waste space between the cells and confers a maximum of mechanical strength on the structure. It is also one of only three figures which fit perfectly together – the other two, the triangle and the square, being quite unsuitable for a cylindrical larva.

For the construction of their nests, Hornets collect rotten wood and also scrape the inner bark from dead and living trees, particularly lilac and ash. The Hornet aligns itself with the wood grain and moves backwards, working fluid into the pulp as it is collected, until a ball the size of its head is formed. Returning to its nest it lays down this pulp in narrow strips, threading it out between the mandibles in a coarse ribbon until the bolus of pulp is used up. The Hornet then reworks the wet mixture into a flatter, more uniform strip, and this dries after a minute or two to form the typical wasp carton. They also incorporate grains of sand or soil into the nest fabric and this produces a carton which is light brown or buff coloured and exceptionally brittle, like badly made paper. The outer layer of the nest is formed of numerous shell-like pockets which give the structure a distinctly scalloped appearance. Eventually this envelope may be 20 cm thick and the whole nest up to 60 cm in diameter. Inside this will be between six and nine cones, and the queen will occupy the lower two to four cones, each suspended by a much thickened mainstay pillar and a variable number of supporting pillars.

Soon up to thirty-nine cells are fashioned by the queen for the emergence of the first worker hornets. During this building phase the queen never feeds and is continually active collecting wood pulp, only stopping occasionally to rest on the spindle above her nest. Next the sausage-shaped eggs are laid and fixed to the cell wall, and these hatch after five days into the larvae which have five development stages or instars, the first three of which occur still attached to the cell. At the end of the fourth instar the developing insect is free in the cell and this larval stage lasts for an average of twelve days during the mid-summer period before a worker Hornet emerges.

Ideally the Hornets' nest is maintained at a temperature of between 29 and 31 °C. This is facilitated by the precise design of the nest and by the generation of heat by the movement of adults and the wriggling of the growing larvae. At night, adult Hornets may mass on the cones to increase the nest temperature, especially around the cones containing brood young, and they manage to maintain a very constant 30°C. If nest temperature increases above the optimum the adults respond by settling at the entrance to the nest and fanning their wings, even aligning themselves to the opening to generate a flow of air into the colony.

Hornets frequently fly on moonlit nights, and frequently visit Sycamore, lime and Wild Angelica to collect energy-rich nectar, but protein-rich arthropods provide the major source of food for the larvae. On location of their prey, Hornets pounce viciously on their victims, knocking them to the ground, and then killing them by biting into their necks, often decapitating the unfortunates within seconds. Only in rare instances do they use their stings when grappling with prey, and then only if it is particularly large or struggling sufficiently to free itself from the Hornet's grasp.

Once immobilized, severing the prey's head, wings and legs is the normal preparatory process before the muscle-filled thorax is carried to a nearby tree and the hunter pumps digestive secretions into its food. The resultant protein-packed soup is stored in its crops and dispensed to the larvae on its return to the nest.

Hornets seldom sting people when they are foraging, unless they are trapped or severely disturbed and it is only if one is tampering with their nest that they can become dangerous. At the entrance several guards will be posted and these will fly as far as seven metres out to examine any strange object. Any intruders, even non-nest members of the same species, are knocked down and stung. Within the venom there is an alarm pheromone, an airborne chemical substance which excites a similar response from other colony members. The venom itself is a mixture of amines and proteins which attacks the cardiovascular system of mammals by reducing blood pressure, preventing coagulation and increasing the permeability of the tissues, resulting in rapid spread of the poison. A strong dose in one sting is calculated to hurt, frighten and thus deter vertebrates. Human deaths as a result of Hornet stings are fortunately few – seventy in the last forty years. Severe allergic responses can result in death and occasionally repeated stings can render a person more susceptible. Then any further stings result in more severe symptoms including unconsciousness, cramp, diarrhoea, nausea and vomiting, the victim finally succumbing to cerebral oedema and convulsions of the heart. Treatment of a person who has been stung consists of removing the sting and washing in soap or antiseptic to prevent secondary infection, then taking an anti-histamine tablet, which should reduce local or general irritation following the sting. All this can be avoided. If you leave these fascinating creatures alone, they will leave you alone.

You have arrived at the sett and made a tremendous din coming through a fence and over a dead tree to try to avoid treading on the Badgers' pathway. You have struck a match, extinguished it, and watched the path of the smoke, and thus have taken a downwind stand on a fallen log while leaning on an old oak pollard. You begin to wait.

The waiting is a form of patient tension. You know you have to wait. You know you will win, so it's not a panic tension. Anticipation rears its head, and the midges bite it off. Frankly, I am immune to any after-effects from such bites. I just get sensationless little red spots for a few hours, which don't itch and then disappear. At the time it is hell. You can't run, you can't hide, you can't even really move. Certainly swiping's out! You try blowing at them, they love it; you try exposing less skin, they flock to the remaining flesh; you try repellant, surely this is actually attracting them! Lastly you slowly wipe your face in a pathetic attempt to reduce its population, they appear to redouble their efforts. Live with the fact that they will always win. One night, the worst ever, my girlfriend counted two hundred and thirty-six red spots on my face alone. If you want to see Badgers in the last rays of daylight you will have to learn to mingle with midges.

These wretched insects belong to the *Ceratopogonidae* and *Simuliidae* families and their attacks are particularly rife in the late evening near sunset, especially if the weather is sultry and the skin therefore perspiring. Especially if you have just walked to a Badger sett. They are commoner in habitats which are suitable for the development of their immature stages, namely aquatic, and the simuliid larvae and pupae demand a degree of aeration of the water not found in stagnant ponds or pools; therefore this species is found

LEFT **A well-used Badger sett**
RIGHT **Woodland at night**

43

around brooks, streams and rivers. It is only the females which bite to provide the necessary food for the development of their eggs. These eggs are often laid in a glutinous mass, on to floating aquatic plants. In some species the females submerge themselves beneath the water, often descending to a considerable depth to lay the eggs. Each of these hatches into a microscopic larva which, with the help of a sucker pad at its rear end, attaches itself to the surface of stones. Nutrition is derived from the tiny particles of debris carried in the current which are sieved out by a series of mouth brushes. The pupa is enclosed within a silken cocoon and as its development proceeds this becomes inflated with an accumulation of gases. What follows is a remarkable birth into the terrestrial world. The pupa, still submerged, splits open and the hairy surface of the now adult fly is enclosed within a bubble of free air. This silvery capsule spirals to the surface where the bubble bursts and the fly immediately takes to its unwetted wings. Vast swarms of males are already waiting over the water and within seconds any female fly has mated!

But enough of these amazing insects. Back at the Badger sett, the ground is glowing orange and some Magpies bark like Bren guns on the edge of the wood. A Blackbird jerks about under the Bracken, and a Bank Vole flicks across the spoil heap without any sound at all. In half an hour it will be twilight, and you will be looking at ghosts instead of badgers. Again you look around the sett. Each hole and its associated spoil heap becomes a precise shape in your mind. A pattern which if subtracted from or added to would scream out a difference. Nothing stirs. There is a noisy silence. Then a faint snapping comes from a huge stand of Bracken and is quickly followed by a whinnying chatter. The rotters have emerged from the other side of the sett, out of view, and a series of vocalizations tells you that some cubs are at play. And that is frustrating. But then a nose and two white stripes stretch elasti-

cally out of the earth really close by. What follows is a precise entrance to the crepuscular world. The slim face, smooth cheeks and narrow neck of a female or sow badger have appeared some eight feet away from you, at about your foot level. She sniffs audibly and pulses further up and out of her silo. All of her weight is on her back legs since she is not keen to commit herself to the open air. Then with a breakdance shuffle she backs down the sand and disappears. You breathe again and release your stranglehold on the tree. What a relief! The tension is broken and you can. . . . The nose reappears, and then much quicker she waddles up the spoil heap and you see her silly little tail for the first time. Simultaneously two more heads appear with less initial caution and fatter features. These are two of her three cubs. They sniff, but are altogether more animated, not so slow as their parent. Heads turn and probe, then all of a rush they barge past her and begin to descend the mound while the sow stands guard over the sett. Now they all jump and freeze, peering down the bank. Stone sentries for seconds, clearly they have heard something you didn't – probably some of their sett cohabitants. Now at last, you become conscious again. The excitement, which was more like fear, fades away and you can study the Badgers as animals, rather than gods demanding the surrender of your senses. Their scale shocks you, they are so small and the cubs are like cuddly, clumsy, monochrome trogs whose amusing waddle develops into a pretty gallop when they appear to run on their toes, never straying from their pathways even when in a panic to bolt back into their clay caverns.

Badgers *Meles meles* are members of the Mustelidae family of small to medium-sized carnivores typified by the weasel, stoat and polecat. There is no difference in colour between the sexes, but they can usually be distinguished in the field by the males' usually more heavy build, broader head, fuller cheeks, shorter head and thick

A Badger sow and two cubs

neck, and somewhat tufty tail, although these characteristics may prove valueless unless a female appears for comparison.

Reproduction is complex in the Badger because mating takes place in every month of the year except November and December, yet cubs are inevitably born in February. This is facilitated by delayed implantation of the embryo in the female's womb, and a variable gestation period. Sows will usually have young in every year, the cubs emerging above ground in April when nine to ten weeks old. They suckle for about twelve weeks, supplementing their diet with any food caught in the sett area, and become independent by fifteen weeks when they are the same size as the adult sows. Female cubs become sexually mature when they are twelve to fifteen months old, but the reasons and mechanism of dispersal of all cubs from their home setts is apparently still a mystery.

Badgers are social animals and live together in groups, called clans, within well-defined areas. They may all inhabit the same sett, or, during particular seasons, occupy neighbouring ones within the home range of the group. Within this group there may well be more than one breeding sow, but the number of adult boars may vary considerably, and the yearling badgers often occupy outlying single-hole setts in the range. Each of these clans will mark the perimeter of their range with dung pits or latrines, and any path which runs between ranges they scent with their sub-caudal glands. These ranges are actively defended for the first four to five months of the year when territorial fighting is frequent. Such vigorous territoriality may lead to regular spacing of the main occupied setts within a given area, provided there is ample food and sites to place the setts. These setts themselves consist of an underground labyrinth of tunnels, often penetrating deep into the ground, and consisting of various chambers, ventilation holes, etc. Cover is a necessary requirement for the siting of setts, because it allows inconspicuous emer-

Backlit Beech

gence: thus ninety-one per cent of the setts recorded in the National Badger Survey of 1971 were in woodland or in other enclosed habitats.

Within the animal kingdom many of the social animals collaborate in the gathering or hunting of food, implying a relationship between food exploitation and the social organisation within species. There are, however, a number of exceptions where group-living animals exploit a food supply for which no cooperation in its exploitation is necessary, and indeed individuals may even interfere with each other. The question thus arises as to the biological function of their social structure. What advantages do they gain from it to establish and maintain it, if hunting is not the reason?

As a gregarious forager the Badger is one such exception, and between 1979 and 1983 my friend, and rampant badger enthusiast, Clive Brown and I made a comprehensive study of the influence of food supply on the ecology of the Badger by studying two populations in southern England. We investigated the influence of food by considering relationships between their social group size and their territory size, and a host of other factors such as prey availability, population density, relative food availability, clan distribution, and other relationships concerning food supply, reproductive activity, body size, and group spacing.

Our two study areas were greatly contrasting; the first, in an urbanized lowland river flood plain, was composed of mostly mixed woodland and dairy pasture; the other, a 16 km square area of the New Forest, was dominated by an ancient deciduous woodland forming an island isolated by heathland. Every week daylight investigations were made of a total of twenty-four setts and outliers, and evening visits were made to count and sex all individuals living in these setts. Hand-held torches, powered by motorcycle batteries and covered with red filters were used successfully after dark without disturbing the animals.

As outlined above, Badgers are territorial animals, and as a means of establishing the sizes of their territories we fed the ever-hungry beggars at their setts with small quantities of peanuts, made sticky with molasses. Cunningly mixed with these peanuts were circular pieces of polythene which were stuck to the mixture by the molasses, and thus consumed by the badgers. Each group in the area was provided with a different colour, and all of the known latrines checked once a week for recovery of the plastic in the faeces. Lovely job! The colour present indicated which clan was maintaining that particular latrine as a territorial marker and thus without even seeing a badger away from the setts we were able to see exactly where they had been and accurately map their territories.

Once a week faeces were collected from both of the study areas and deep frozen for subsequent analysis which resulted in lengthy evenings in a lonely laboratory sieving, filtering and then peering through the microscope at the badger dung. Another lovely job! By the end of 1983 a lot of concise data had been gathered. The dung results showed that earthworms were the most important dietary component in both of the study areas and indeed the Badgers were a kind of earthworm specialist feeders, actively exploiting relatively richer habitats proportionally to the density of worms found in those habitats. This overwhelming dependence on a single prey item had marked effects on our

Badgers' ecology. In areas where a high earthworm density was seen, such as in the pasture fields in the river valley, the badgers were very territorial and regulated their group size by the earthworm availability in the rigid territories. Here high densities of Badgers were found and each of the clans produced cubs in each year. In the New Forest, where earthworm densities are much lower due to a higher percentage of coniferous woodland and heathland, the Badgers were much more reliant on other dietary components taken when they were encountered, such as fruits, beetles, fungi and even the occasional bird or mammal. This resulted in the badgers being almost entirely non-territorial. Here the badger densities were significantly lower and only half of the Badger clans had young in each year. From this it would appear that earthworm availability directly affects the breeding capability of Badger clans and thus, to some degree, regulates the clan size.

Actual litter size was the same in both areas, however, so the difference in breeding success was not due to a variation in the size of the litter, a mechanism used by many animals, but in control of the actual number of litters in each clan. In a mammal such as the Badger, where reproduction is advanced and complex, it is likely that this type of regulation is physiologically impossible. Actual loss of young is more likely to be caused by food stress, where body fat reserves are not large enough to complete gestation and lactation.

So, simplistically if you are a Badger, food availability within your territory controls your group size. But why live in a group anyway? Wouldn't you be better off with a monogamous wife and cubs in your own territory? Actually, no. Since the food supply is patchy and unpredictable, due to climatic effects on earthworm emergence, large exclusive areas are needed to guarantee continual food availability and such an area is best defended by a group. One individual could not profitably patrol the perimeter necessary to enclose the patches. As more members are admitted to the group the cost to the group of border defence gets larger as the area needed to support them increases, but proportionally smaller to each individual and thus a benefit of group living is achieved. Other factors are involved, including access to females, providing for other cubs and almost certainly kinship, as clan members are likely to be closely related.

However, in the New Forest such territory–group–food relationships were nonexistent, due to the very low densities of earthworms present. Here, to maintain exclusive ranges large enough to provide food for the whole clan is impossible since they would have to overlap drastically with the other ranges, and could not in any case be maintained by the latrine method of demarcation. The perimeters would be so large that the Badgers would have to have a severe and continued attack of diarrhoea in order to mark them! The low availability of worms also affected the distribution of the animals, and they were considerably more scattered than their counterparts in the other study area. This was especially so in winter when the food supply may have been reduced due to unfavourable foraging conditions. In order to forage more effectively this population had divided itself into smaller groups with little bond to any one sett, making continual use of the more abundant outliers and even abandoning their main setts. This behaviour may reduce competition with other individuals and has led to a breakdown of the clan system seen elsewhere.

What a lot of effort to at first understand and then to explain isolated fragments of an animal's lifestyle. Think of this while waiting for your Badgers and watch a hundred hungry gnats, backlit behind the trees. Burning, sparkling and swirling for minutes. They burn so brightly, they are so entertaining, so simple and yet so beautiful. Each one an invaluable component of the mass, a separate sparkle of living light. If you wait long enough the sun will set and the glade will be poorer.

7. RUTTING, ROTTERS AND TO CAP IT ALL, DEATH!

Whenever I have been to see Fallow Deer rutting it has been raining, or rather drizzling. Fine drizzle which completely soaks your coat, your hair, your binoculars and your camera. Everything is wet. The trees drip and the wood seems to smell so damp you can taste it. The fungi love it. An array of their toadstool fruiting bodies appears so colourful in the greyness of the leaf litter. If you kneel to examine the fungi, these leaves stick tight to your knees and hands, but because of their wetness and your numbness you cannot peel them off. Your fingers wrinkle and there are no sharp sounds. Drizzle dampens the world. But it does little to dampen the spirits of the deer.

To them the rut is a form of sexual extravaganza, a continual carnival of activity which, like much of that seen in the animal kingdom, has a tendency to violence. It occurs at the beginning of the breeding season when the intense sexual behaviour of the males, or bucks, sets them in contest to decide a mating order for the aggregated females, or does. Basically this behaviour is initiated by the effects of increased male hormone production. Amongst other things this also stimulates the development of antlers, which are used as a visual stimulus to determine social standing or, if this fails, for fighting.

These paired, branched and bony protuberances are restricted to males in deer, as opposed to horns which are unbranched permanent structures which may be carried by females as well as males. Horns are composed of a living core of bone covered in true horn, which is similar in composition to human fingernails and which continually grows at the base and unlike antlers both the bony core and the horny covering are retained throughout the life of the animal. Antlers grow from bony pedicles arising from the frontal bones on the skull, and while growing they are covered in a soft hairy skin,

LEFT **Fallow Bucks**
RIGHT **Sulphur-tuft Fungus**

known as velvet. When their growth is completed at the end of August this skin dies and is shed, leaving a bare antler composed solely of dead bone. Such newly grown antler, stripped of its velvet, is rough and pale. but it soon becomes smoother and acquires a characteristic brown colour. This is attributed to blood staining and to juices from the vegetation against which the antler is rubbed to remove the velvet.

Antlers vary greatly in size during the buck's life, ranging from small knobs or spikes in yearling deer to large branched structures in mature animals. Palmation is only seen in Fallow Deer and, unlike antlers of most species of deer, these are very much wider at the top than at the bottom. The well-developed forward-pointing points, or brow tines, leave the main beam just above the antlers' base, or coronet, and the broad palm usually curves inwards at the top, often having many small back-pointing projections called spellers. Palmation develops from the second year onwards and a buck's antlers become larger and more palmated with increasing age until he reaches his prime, usually in his eighth or ninth year. The total length of the antler may reach 70 cm and the length of the palm about 40 cm, and a pair of antlers may attain a weight of about 4 kilograms. The threat of injury from such imposing weapons has led to a thickening of the skin on the forehead between the antler pedicles. This thickens by up to a centimetre during the autumn, giving a greater resistance against knocks and no doubt preventing more serious injury to the underlying skull during any fighting.

Besides antlers other secondary sexual characteristics develop in time for the rut, namely the loud belching voice, a pungent rutting odour, a large increase in the girth of the neck and eversion and brown staining of the end of the penis sheath.

During late August and September the Fallow bucks move from their summer grounds, which are often far from those of the female herd, and arrive at the rutting stands, which may be used year after year.

Clues to the presence of a rutting stand are scrapes in the ground and thrashed and frayed bushes and trees. The scrapes are made by bucks pawing at the ground with their forefeet and scraping their antlers, and may be as little as 30 cm or as much as 3 m in diameter. Once a scrape has been formed, the buck sometimes adds his pungent-smelling urine, and some of this mixed with soil may be transferred to his body by his antlers. The damage to trees and shrubs may make deer unpopular with the forester; it occurs when bucks attack saplings repeatedly with their antlers, whole branches often being broken off and scattered about. Young elder bushes and willow trees are particular targets, but almost any tree may be attacked and this behaviour reaches its peak in the second half of October, the height of the rut.

This rut 'proper' is a period of extraordinary activity. A rutting buck parades up and down his territory groaning frequently and continually chivvying the does, and their fawns, who have been attracted to him. His life is complicated by a number of males which hang around on the edge of this herd. These may be tolerated to a surprising extent, but if two bucks attempt to rut in the same area a fight often occurs. Heads are lowered so the crown and antlers are presented to the opponent and, with noses pointing at the ground, the combat begins. Repeated head-on clashes are rarely seen; disagreements are largely shoving matches with antlers locked, the loud thrashing and clashing resulting from tine striking tine as the two opponents twist, buckle and manoeuvre in the soft rain-soaked ground. The heaving deer exhibit tremendous power as they push each other backwards and forwards, until the weaker is forced to flee.

Triumphant, the victor groans. Having scored his assailant's flank with his antlers, he opens his mouth and lifts his head so his forehead is almost horizontal, antlers swept back and the larynx dropping considerably down his throat. Each belch lasts about one second, and he may give up to 150 groans in four minutes, each blasting a breath of stale steam into the damp, autumn air.

Does show a variety of interest in these proceedings, ranging from completely ignoring their rampant master by continuing to rest and graze, skipping away as he approaches, or standing their ground while he wipes his various scent glands on their flanks. Standing does are often sniffed and licked in the anal area and a curious piece of behaviour exhibited by many ungulates called 'flehemen' occurs after the male has savoured the female's urine. He raises his head, curls back the upper lip and drops the lower one, and this whole, rather distasteful process is probably designed to test whether the female is on heat. Actual mating may occur well away from the rutting territory. Courtship involves the buck chasing the doe with head and neck stretched forward. She may lie with the head and neck stretched along the ground, sometimes pointing the head vertically in response to his caress, but when she is ready to be mated she stands and allows the buck to mount and copulate.

Far off in the forthcoming June a single fawn will be born from this culmination of the rut; a little bundle of spotted chestnut will be bothered by flies as it struggles, shaking, to stand in the lush Bracken and warm sunshine. Now, though, the satiated buck turns and strides away, belching into the mist, breathing in the air of decomposition which has risen in the woods.

FOREST FUNERAL DIRECTORS

The time of the rut is also the time of the decomposers, one of the most important groups of which are the fungi. My favourites are the huge fungal conurbations which appear out of cut or broken stumps. Clumps of Honey Fungus *Armillarea mellea*, Beech Tuft *Oudemansiella mucida* and *Gymnopilus junonius* arise like models of a space city for a cheap American 1960s science fiction movie. Cities of water without being iced, masses

Sulphur-tuft Fungus

of perfect parasols overlying each other, candy castles which are soft and defenceless against all but the lightest of rains. They grow like empires gaining in volume and strength and then decay just as quickly, losing form and reason until they melt into a huge amorphous brown slimy mass which is washed away drip by drip, to dissolve in the soil which seemed to spawn it. Individually, in their prime they are perfect. Each gill is perfectly aligned and so clean, so pure of colour, so sharp. Like impossibly crafted porcelain razors arranged in a circle under a velvety cap, and supported by a rod of striated sugar. Some are as translucent as the tenderest blooms of any flower, but in a way they are more miraculous: their beauty can sprout from stinking and rotting soils and substrates.

Indeed, in trying to understand the life forms of fungi it is best to begin again and not even try to compare them to plants or animals. Fungi have no chlorophyll for photosynthesis. Many are saprophytic, secreting enzymes into the surrounding material, which is usually dead, which are able to break down a wide range of compounds in the rotting material. This chemically rich soup is then reabsorbed by the fungi and provides them with their essential nutrients.

Fungi reproduce by spores and not seeds. These measure about 1/1000th of a millimetre in diameter and differ from seeds in that they are not a highly organized structure, they lack an embryo and consist of only an outer cell wall enclosing a fragment of protoplasm and a little food material. In toadstool types of fungi, these spores are actively discharged into the air space between the gills so they can fall by gravity, aided by an electrostatic charge that is present between adjacent gills. Once free of the fruiting body, spores can be dispersed either by rain or wind. Phenomenal numbers are produced. In a giant puffball there can be as many as 7×10^{12} in total and a bracket fungus can release 3×10^{10} per day for six months of the year. Spores do not formally germinate like the seeds of green plants, they just extend until they become a thread-like tube, which then spreads in a long, thin, continuous growth called a hypha.

An individual hypha may live for up to a week and when it gets longer and more branched it is called a mycelium. Unlike plants and animals which have separate cells, in fungi the protoplasm is continuous through every cell in the body, throughout the whole of the organism. Generally a fungal mycelium has no particular shape but it can organize itself, by massing the hyphae together into fruit bodies such as toadstools. These capped structures are designed to keep the underlying gills free of water and their ability to grow rapidly is well known. They can, in fact, double their volume every two hours. Such growth is confined to cell elongation which is only

possible through a massive intake of water. Most hyphae are composed of ninety per cent water and thus fungi in general are very sensitive to desiccation, this being the major cause of their death and the reason why they are more visibly prolific in our damp autumns.

As much as all the green plants are important for their massive production of material, decomposers such as the fungi are equally important, since if they were not present in the ecosystem processes of decay would be non-existent or incredibly slow. All the nutrients would remain locked in the dead plant material and the essential cycling of materials could not function. Within our woodlands there are 6,000 different species of fungi, each growing in its particular niche determined by the presence of particular host species.

The famous Fly Agaric *Amanita muscaria* with its bright scarlet cap, covered in white or yellowish warts, and white gills and stem is usually found amongst birches and under pines. It is quite unmistakable since it is normally known from earliest childhood as the typical fairy-tale mushroom. It is poisonous, and the symptoms may consist of colic, vomiting, diarrhoea, accompanied by delirium, loss of memory, convulsions and prostration with a tendency to sleep. The alkaloid poison resides principally in the skin of the cap and the name Fly Agaric comes from the former practice of breaking the cap up in milk in order to stupefy house flies. This method was still used in Rumania, Czechoslovakia and Poland until fairly recently. There is also a legend that this fungus was the drug used to deliberately craze Viking berserkers before they went into battle as axe-wielding madmen.

Actual deaths attributed to fungus poisoning are almost invariably related to the Death Cap *A. phalloides*, the Fool's Mushroom *A. verna* and the Destroying Angel *A. virosa*. The infamous Death Cap has a flattened greenish-olive silky cap, with blackish fibrils radiating from the centre. Occasionally it may be yellow or brownish,

Porcelain fungus

or even whitish, and the gills and the stem are white, often with a greeny tinge. It has no particular smell or taste and is most frequently found after the first summer rains in open areas in woods and their adjoining pastures, where it continues to appear until early autumn. The Fool's Mushroom closely resembles the Death Cap but is usually entirely white; and, similarly coloured, the Destroying Angel has a viscid cap which is often asymmetrical. Both are rare, but can be found in summer and autumn under beech trees.

Deaths from Death Cap poisoning are horrific. After ingestion there is an incubation period of ten to twelve hours when no discomfort is felt. This is followed by sudden and intense abdominal pains with vomiting, cold sweats, diarrhoea and excessive thirst. These conditions subside after a couple of days, but this period of a few hours' quiescence is most dangerous, because afterwards the symptoms return in a much more intense form. The nervous system is gradually paralysed, the liver degenerates and there is delirium, followed by collapse, coma and then death. This gruesome finale occurs three to ten days after ingestion, depending upon the resistance of the victim and the amount of fungus absorbed. All parts of the fungus, the spores, the cap and the stem are dangerous and, surprisingly, a very small amount will cause illness or even death. At the Pasteur Institute in Paris they have produced an anti-phallodian serum by immunizing horses, and this is a most effective cure if it is injected shortly after the first signs of poisoning. It can be despatched at short notice from the Institute if a case of poisoning is suspected, but altogether I would suggest that any budding fungal foragers leave this species to the slugs and snails which seem immune to its diabolical consequences. Indeed, it is probably best not to eat any fungus, whether raw or cooked, unless it is conclusively identified as edible by an expert. This also prevents the indigestion caused by eating inconclusively identified fungi.

8. THE PRICE IS ABSCISSION

A bed of Bracken in October. A corroded tangle of copper and bronze and alloys of yellow and green in a ceaseless vermiculate chaos of decay. The ferns have formed, finished and now they're falling. Their colour in soft light is enveloping and soothing, in mist it's like a dream, a dirge where form is lost and the Bracken beds become just muted colour. In the yellow, autumn sun such a spread becomes a smouldering array where every little dying leaflet is separated and sharpened. Beneath them those once strong stems now buckle and snap under the weight of their dried leaves. They are hollow, sapless tubes which are as brittle as bones and snap as easily. In rain they wane softly, seemingly painlessly and you cannot hear them falling. On a dry morning if you startle a Roe buck, and he prances away, they crash as they smash and then crackle and pop. Then he stops and they stop. Then he walks and they rustle away with him. But it's not only colour and sound. An earthy dull and damp smell of rich decay, which excites the bacteria and soil-bound decomposers, pervades the wood.

Above the Bracken the leaves of the chestnut are reeling, twisting, dancing, swimming and spinning down. The wood's gone cold, got old and gone gold. No sooner have they died than the wind whips the chestnut's children up into a chaos of movement and dry sound. It's autumn and the chestnut leaves flee the tree and throng to the ground.

During the summer, conditions were suitable for productive photosynthesis, and the tree was able to utilize its leaves efficiently. Water needed for photosynthesis is pulled by a process called transpiration up to the leaves from the roots. Without this evaporational phenomenon fluids could never reach the top of an oak tree, but by actively breathing, through millions of pores called stomata in the

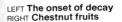

LEFT **The onset of decay**
RIGHT **Chestnut fruits**

leaves' surfaces, the plant can in theory draw water up to a height of over 1 kilometre. This is possible due to the forces of adhesion between the water molecules and the molecules comprising the material lining the vascular tubes, which run from root to leaf in the plant. Once established this column of water is prevented from breaking by the forces of attraction between like molecules, the force of cohesion. These two physical forces are enough to drive transpiration and living plant cells are not required. In summer the bright light encourages the stomata to open, and wind, higher temperature and humidity can cause massive losses of water from plants. Indeed, an oak tree may transpire as much as 680 litres of water in one day. In winter trees could not afford this sort of water loss as it is very scarce, imprisoned as snow and ice out of the trees' reach, and because bright light still opens the pores in the leaves and increases water loss, a mechanism has developed to prevent dehydration. This is leaf-shedding or abscission.

At the end of summer the leaf enters a phase of senescence. The rate of photosynthesis declines, there is a gradual fall in chlorophyll and proteins, and the chloroplasts become disorganized, the cells' nuclei degenerate and all the essential mineral elements are translocated out of the dying leaves. Concurrently the processes that facilitate abscission are in operation. At the base of the leaf-stalk a layer of cells begins to change their morphology. They become thinner, parts dissolve and separation proceeds from the outside of the stalk inwards until the leaf only remains attached by the woody vascular tissues in the centre of the stalk. This fragile bond is eventually broken by the wind and the leaf falls. The scale of abscission can be enormous. Between October and December three tonnes of leaves per hectare are shed on to the woodland floor. By March only a third remains. The rest has been processed by the decomposers.

The numbers of these organisms is staggering. If there are seventy-five oak trees in a hectare there are 300,000 million soil nematode worms. One square metre contains millions of bacteria and 100×10^7 mites, springtails, amoebae, rotifers,

Maple leaf-skeletons

A woodlouse – our woodland crustacean

eelworms, enchytraid worms, earthworms, millipedes, false scorpions, slugs and snails. The competition between this array is intense. Fungi are grazed by nematodes and protozoa which are in turn the prey of other fungi, and the overall outcome is a very rapid breakdown of the dead plant tissues into raw nutrients. Nitrogen, sulphur, phosphorus, calcium, magnesium and iron all appear in the humus and actual rates of decay are influenced by the moisture level, frost action, the soil structure and the particular assemblage of litter species present. There is an order of decomposition whereby the largest animals such as earthworms process the material first and their waste is in turn processed by smaller organisms until the remaining polysaccharide gums, fats and waxes are finally attacked by the bacteria and reduced to their component parts.

WOODLAND CRABS

One of my favourite decomposers is the indefatigable woodlouse *Oniscus* sp. About forty-two different species of woodlouse can be found in the British Isles, *of* which twenty-nine may be indigenous, the most familiar species being *Oniscus assellus*, *Porcellio scaber* and *Philoscia muscorum*. Woodlice are more closely related to crabs, lobsters and waterfleas than any insects, since they are one of the few groups of land-living Crustacea. They are Isopods, a group which is better designed for walking than swimming. They are thought to have evolved from ancestors which began walking on the sea-bed and then, via intertidal species, became more terrestrial than marine, and about 160 million years ago settled for life on land. They were well prepared for this by having strong skeletons to support their body tissues, sturdy legs for rapid loco-motion, chewing rather than filtering mouthparts and internal fertilization. The development of a brood pouch to hold the developing young protected them from desiccation, and this meant that they did not need to return to water to breed. But this desiccation is also their one great handicap. It has damned them to live in the damp, dark and dank surroundings of rotting wood, because they lack the water-proof skin of the insects and breathe using modified gills which lose a lot of water.

Woodlice have a characteristic low-slung stance which gives them tremen-dous stability. Their seven pairs of legs develop great power to push the animal through the rotting substrate. In some species such as *Philoscia muscorum* the legs have developed into longer forms more suitable for rapid escape. *O. asellus*, having a flattened body, grips its substrate very tightly like a limpet shell and is very difficult to prise off. Pill bugs are known for their ability to roll up in a ball and, once they are tight shut, animals such as shrews *Sorex* spp. find it impossible to find a purchase with their jaws and end up frus-trated, pushing the pill bug around with their twitching noses.

Woodlouse mating takes place in total darkness and thus, like dormouse and Woodcock behaviour, has only recently been observed. When a male finds a receptive female he tests the air with rapid movements of his antennae before bring-ing them to rest on the female. If she does not run off he climbs on her back, licking her head with his mouthparts and drum-ming on her carapace with his front legs. After five minutes of this he performs an amazing feat of contortion, bending his body diagonally under the female to pres-ent his left-hand genitalia to her right-hand genitalia. After several minutes or so he swaps sides and repeats this stunt before shuffling off into the darkness. Next the female stops feeding and becomes inac-tive. A few days later she moults her skin, tail end first, and often eats this whitish

husk to conserve nutrients. Simulta-neously, she develops a brood pouch which forms a false floor to her body. This fills with liquid and receives the fertilized eggs. Eventually, when they are ready, the young crawl out of this pouch but they suf-fer a very high mortality because they are less able to prevent desiccation than the adults. At times there can be as many as 2,000 woodlice per square metre in wood-land, all feeding avidly on dead material and sharing the burden of primary decom-position with earthworms and millipedes. They in turn form part of the diets of shrews, toads, Slow Worms, some beetles and a spider *Dysdera crocata*, which has specialized in woodlouse feeding. Brownish-red and only a centimetre long, it has formidable jaws with which it seizes woodlice in a pincer-like grip before pois-oning them in less than seven seconds.

WINTER WILDERNESS

December. The sun is yellow and weak and the shadows are long, the wood becomes a naked cage with boughs for bars. The chestnut trees look saddened, like pensioners ridden of joy. In spring they sprouted their sticky buds and seemingly sang with the birds and beasts in a giants' chorus. In summer they flowered white and pink candles and then showered them over the darkened floor. They were full of form and proud. Now they scream at night and the beasts scowl. Then it will snow and the timber will become metallized. Hard as steel and as cold and as brutal. The frost will split them and the winds rip them up. For me a winter wood at night is hard and aggressive. It's been slashed and simpli-fied. It's now a ghost town, only an echo of its former glory, a kingdom passed under the curse of time.

Go for a walk in a winter wood in hard frost or snow. It's so open and bright. A monochromatic white and sepia brown and black. The sounds, which would have been muffled by ten million leaves in the summer, echo sharp and loud through the blasted ruins. You can see further and hear

A winter wilderness

further, yet the songs of the warblers and the Redstarts are now delivered in Africa, and the hum of the Hornet is reduced to an inaudible tick in the cells of a hibernating queen, hidden in the crevice of an old oak.

A similar silence exudes from the giant larvae of the Stag Beetle locked in a decaying stump for five years. He may scrape or twitch occasionally if a squirrel hops on to his log, torn from its torpor by a lull in the seasonal severity, to leap about looking for its too well hidden caches of nuts. The dormouse sleeps in the pleasant smell of Honeysuckle lining its log-bound nest and steam rises slowly from a Badger's hole into the crisp air, to betray residency of the sett. Treecreepers and Nuthatches join up with the tits in flocks which circuit the woodland in a feeding frenzy. Up and down the trunks they forage, requiring a hidden insect every few seconds to justify their activity, let alone to live. They may find a few caterpillars or pupae, like those of the White Admiral wrapped in its Honeysuckle hovel, but the cryptic Purple Emperor survives, hidden in its Sallow cleft.

A Woodcock erupts from a seeping stream and bullets off over a herd of dark-looking Fallow does, who skip away through the trunks to scrape at the bulbs of Bluebells. Deep in these tubers a collection of cells fizzles, just. The detonator for development, since although some species have migrated, or hibernated, or regressed, or senesced in this time of inertness, this ecosystem is a capsule under a spell, gently and surely ticking. Spring breaks the spell, and the capsule's potential is magnificent. It's a spectacle. It will not grow so much as explode into the most diverse, dynamic, rich and interesting of our earthly habitats. Woodland – the competitive and complex climax of communal life.

Identification of what is around you will greatly increase your enjoyment of Natural History. The following pages describe some of the species that are most likely to be encountered in a woodland habitat. Each species is also featured in a colour plate, representative of the type of habitat in which it is most likely to be found. The combination of the picture and description should enable you to find out what is flying, standing, buzzing or growing in front of you. Unless otherwise stated all the measurements are, in the case of flowers, heights or, in the case of animals, lengths.

Woodland Residents ~ A GUIDE

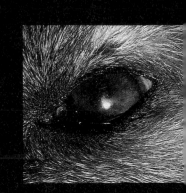

LEFT **The classic outline of Bracken**
RIGHT **The eye of a Fox**

SUMMER

THE SEASON OF DECAY

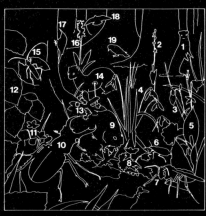

THE FLOOR OF THE WOOD

1 Weasel (p. 95)
2 Fly Orchid (p. 78)
3 Columbine (p. 73)
4 Snowdrops (p. 80)
5 Lords and Ladies (p. 78)
6 Cardinal Beetle (p. 84)
7 Hornet (p. 83)
8 Wood Anemone (p. 73)
9 Bank Vole (p. 95)
10 Stag Beetle (p. 85)
11 Wood Sorrel (p. 74)
12 Common Beech (p. 72)
13 Primrose (p. 80)
14 Stoat (p. 95)
15 Longhorn Beetle (p. 84)
16 Early Purple Orchid (p. 80)
17 Treecreeper (p. 89)
18 Woodpigeon (p. 90)
19 Jay (p. 89)

THE WOODLAND AT NIGHT

1 Noctule Bat (p. 95)
2 Long-eared Owl (p. 87)
3 Common Long-eared Bat (p. 95)
4 Tawny Owl (p. 87)
5 Red Fox (p. 95)
6 Enchanter's Nightshade (p. 74)
7 Woodruff (p. 75)
8 Yellow-necked Mouse (p. 91)
9 Wood Mouse (p. 91)
10 Goldilocks Buttercup (p. 80)
11 Ramsons (p. 76)
12 Badger (p. 92)
13 Silver Birch (p. 72)

WOODLAND WARBLERS

1 Goshawk (p. 86)
2 Spotted Flycatcher (p. 88)
3 Sparrowhawk (p. 86)
4 Chinese Water Deer (p. 94)
5 Red Deer (p. 93)
6 Wood Warbler (p. 88)
7 Willow Warbler (p. 88)
8 Common Hazel (p. 72)
9 Chiffchaff (p. 88)
10 Purple Hairstreak (p. 83)
11 Narrow-leaved Helleborine (p. 77)
12 Greater Butterfly Orchid (p. 78)
13 Broad-leaved Helleborine (p. 77)
14 Foxglove (p. 80)
15 Great Spotted Woodpecker (p. 87)
16 Pied Flycatcher (p. 88)

PLANTS

Silver Birch *Betula pendula* 25 m
This tree is easily recognized by its papery, black and white, peeling bark, the trunk being rugged at its base and the shining brown twigs supporting alternate very pointed oval leaves. Yellowish catkins are found in April, the fruits are dispensed in July, and this tree is widespread and common in woods, on light sandy and gravelly soils, especially in the south.

Hornbeam *Carpinus betulus* 30 m
This is a neat, often smallish deciduous native tree, which is widespread but only frequent in south-east England, especially in oak-woods. It flowers in April or May, has loose hanging catkins and later small nutlike fruits. The pointed oval leaves are toothed and rather like hazel, but with a narrower head and hairy main veins on the underside of the leaf.

Common Hazel *Corylus avellana* 6 m
This is a tall deciduous native shrub, which if coppiced may live for many years. In spring the pale lemon yellow hanging male catkins are very characteristic and the erect budlike female catkins have bright red styles. These develop into the nuts which are held in a jaggedly toothed husk and appear between September and October. The leaves are pointed oval and toothed and at first are downy on both sides. This shrub is common throughout the British Isles.

Common Beech *Fagus sylvatica* 40 m
This deciduous native may live for up to 200 years and is found most commonly on chalk limestone and well drained loams and sands. It is a lofty tree with a massive round trunk and smooth grey bark. Its leaves are pointed oval, waxy and tender green when young, later hairy only on the veins beneath. The male flowers are in a short tassel and soon fall. The fruit, or mast, is a copper-brown three-sided nut encased in a tough bristly husk.

Pendunculate or English Oak
Quercus robur 30 m
Sessile Oak *Q. petraea* 30 m
Both of these trees are deciduous natives and may live for up to 800 years or more. The Pendunculate Oak occurs on rich lowland soils in Britain and flowers in May, giving acorns in October. The leaves are oblong, commonly broad at their base, lobed and paler beneath, being hairless when mature. This is what distinguishes the species from the Sessile Oak which has leaves tapering to the unlobed base on longer stalks and is still downy on the underside when mature. This species is also widespread, but especially on the acid soils of the north and the west and on the light sandy soils in the south and east. The acorn of this species sits on the twig, whilst on the Penduculate Oak it is supported on a long stalk, called a penduncle.

Common Lime *Tilia europaea*
Small-leaved Lime *T. cordata*
The Common Lime has heartshaped dark green leaves which are hairless above and paler below. Its flowers are yellowish, heavily scented and hang in umbel-like clusters and form globular, downy, ribbed fruits. This species is almost always planted and only occasionally found in hedges and copses away from houses. It forms a fertile hybrid with the Small-leaved Lime, which is distinguished by its smaller leaves, being greyish below marked with feint side veins and tufts of reddish hair. This species is widespread but local in woods occurring more frequently on limestone.

Common Ash *Fraxinus excelsior* 25 m
This species is widespread and common in woods, especially on limestone. It flowers in April and May before it leaves. Flowers appear as tufts of purplish black stamens soon turning greenish. Fruits are winged and hang in clumps until October and November. Often the last to leaf, the buds are black and the leaves opposite and pinnate with long leaflets.

A glade of Foxgloves

Wood Anemone
Anemone nemorosa 8–15 cm

This species occurs throughout the British Isles, being only absent from unwooded areas of eastern England and some Scottish isles. It is most abundant on acid or waterlogged soils in woodland, especially in coppices. Its graceful solitary white flowers 2.5 cm across have numerous yellow anthers and sometimes a pink or purple tinge beneath. These appear in spring after which the leaves soon wither. The flowers produce no nectar, but pollination is effected by bees, bumble bees and flies. A low perennial it may carpet many woodlands with its much divided trifoliate leaves and it is an indicator of ancient woodland.

Columbine *Aquilegia vulgaris* 60–90 cm

This species is now local and decreasing, yet it occurs throughout Britain, as far north as southern Scotland, in damp woodlands often on calcareous soils. It is easily recognized by its dark violet-blue or white flowers which have five tubular petals, the spurs of which are short and curved back with sepals of the same colour. These flowers appear during May and June and the nectar produced at the base of the long spur is collected by long-tongued bumble bees. Usually hairless, it has slightly greyish trifoliate root leaves. Also a popular garden plant, escapees may now be established but can be distinguished from the endemic species by their rose pink or paler coloured flowers.

Common Dog-violet *Viola riviniana* 12 cm

By far the commonest wild violet this species has heart-shaped leaves, as broad as long, placed on a non-central flowering rosette. Between April and June its blue-violet flowers with overlapping petals appear, these having a stout curved creamy coloured spur notched at the tip. The appendages of the sepals enlarge when the plant is in fruit. It occurs throughout the British Isles where it grows on both acid and calcareous soils but avoids water-logged conditions. It could be confused with other violet species, such as Wood Dog Violet *Viola reichenbachiana*, Hairy Violet *V. hirta* and Sweet Violet *V. odorata*.

Wood Sorrel *Oxalis acetosella* 5–10 cm
This delicate, creeping perennial has tufts of root leaves and solitary flowers measuring 1 cm across, which are usually veined mauve standing on taller leafless stalks up to 10 cm high. It prefers well-drained woodland soils and is very shade tolerant, being widespread and common throughout almost all of the British Isles. In parts of England it can be used as an indicator to ancient woodland, and it may also grow as an epiphyte. It flowers in the spring and is self-pollinating.

Enchanter's Nightshade
Circaea lutetiana 15–30 cm
This downy perennial is a nightshade in name alone and is nothing like the true nightshades (the Deadly and Woody

Nightshades of the Nightshade family Solanaceae) but belongs to the willowherb family Onagraceae. It has gently toothed, pointed oval or heart-shaped leaves. The flowers, which appear from June to August, are set on leafless spikes and are tiny and white, with two notched petals sometimes being tinged pink. After insect pollination the fruits are club-shaped and cling to clothes with their thick covering of tiny hooked bristles. This plant is widespread throughout the whole of the British Isles as far north as central Scotland where it is common in woodlands and coppice on moist soils. It is also very shade tolerant.

Dog's Mercury
Mercurialis perennis 10–30 cm
This species is distributed throughout the whole of the British Isles, but is rare in northern Scotland and Ireland. It is abundant in deciduous woodlands and old hedgerows, where it is very tolerant of shade, yet sensitive to waterlogging. In beech-woods it can completely dominate

Horse Chestnuts

Beech nuts

the ground vegetation where it forms extensive carpets. A creeping perennial it has separate male and female plants which flower from February to April. There are between one and three flowers occurring together on stalks which lengthen as the hairy fruits ripen. The stems are unbranched and rather leafless below, but dark green broad lanceolate toothed opposite leaves and smallish green petal less flowers occur which in the male are on long prominent spikes. It is wind pollinated.

Wood Spurge
Euphorbia amygdaloides 30 cm
This downy, unbranched perennial has narrow lanceolate leaves often tinged red and unusual flowers with converging horns on their lobes. These flowers appear between March and May and produce fruits which are almost smooth. It is a plant of southern England occurring in most of the country as far north as The Wash, and may be especially common following the clearance of a coppiced woodland. It is also an indicator of ancient woodlands.

Deadly Nightshade
Atropa belladonna 0.6-2 m
This tall, stout, bushy perennial flowers from June to August and occurs most frequently south and east of a line from the Tyne to the Severn, where it is primarily a plant of woodland clearings and paths. It has pointed oval stalked leaves and at the base of these solitary, large, drooping and bell-shaped purple flowers. These develop into glossy black berries the size of a small cherry surrounded by the bright green calyx lobes. The most infamous of our poisonous plants, all parts of this species are toxic. The poison is an alkaloid, and the most poisonous parts are the roots and berries, small amounts of which are lethal.

Woodruff *Galium odoratum* 15-30 cm
This fragrant perennial has slightly shiny

Ramsons

leaves, edged with minute forward pointed prickles, arranged in whorls of six to nine up the unbranched stem. On its favoured moist, rich, base or calcareous soils it will carpet the woodland floor, where it flowers during May and June. These flowers are small and white in loose heads, and the fruits produced are small with hooked bristles. It is widely distributed throughout the British Isles, except for some north western isles, but is less common in Scotland and Ireland.

Common Solomon's Seal *Polygonatum multiflorum* 30–90 cm

This is a local species, commonest in central southern England, but it occurs elsewhere in England and Wales. It prefers dry woodlands especially on chalk, where between June and July it sends flowers dangling from its round arching stems, with broad erect and elliptical alternate leaves. These flowers hang in clusters of one to three, and are small white and

waisted barrel-like structures. Pollination by bumble bees results in a black berry.

Yellow Star of Bethlehem *Gagea lutea* 8–24 cm

This species occurs throughout England and southern Scotland, but is local in its distribution, most often occurring in damp woodlands on deep, rich calcareous soils. A bulbous and hairless perennial it has leaves much like the Bluebell, but they are more yellow than green and more hooded at the tip, with three prominent ridged veins on the back instead of one. Flowering occurs from March to May and the yellowish-green flowers occur in umbel-like clusters, often quite sparingly. Pollination is by insects, producing three-sided fruits.

Ramsons *Allium ursinum* 30 cm

This bulbous perennial forms spectacular carpets in spring. Its broad leaves', resembling Lily-of-the-valley, major characteristic is their smell which is of a rich onionygarlic. The flower stalks are three-sided and bear a broad umbel of long-stalked, white flowers with narrow, pointed petals. It flowers from April to June and is self-pollinated, the fruits being tri-lobed. This species favours damp woodlands on rich loamy soils throughout England and Wales, but is distributed throughout the British Isles being less common in north-east Scotland and rather local in Ireland.

Herb Paris *Paris quadrifolia* 30 cm

This hairless perennial has an unbranched stem which is leafless except at the top. Here four, large, unstalked, pointed, oval leaves appear below the curious flower whose four very narrow, green petals are slightly shorter than the four lanceolate, green sepals, and a little larger than the eight erect, green stamens which have yellow anthers. These are topped by a purplish berry which is crowned by the four styles, and this weird structure makes this plant quite unmistakable and unusual. Herb Paris flowers between May and August and is pollinated by small flies. It is a locally frequent species, distributed throughout most of England, but rare in Wales and Scotland. It favours damp limestone woodlands, often growing with Dog's Mercury, and is an indicator of ancient woodland.

Red Helleborine
Cephalanthera rubra 30 cm
Violet Helleborine
Epipactis purpurata 50 cm
Broad-leaved Helleborine
Epipactis Helleborine 60 cm
Narrow-leaved Helleborine
Cephalanthera longifolia 60 cm

These four woodland helleborine species are easily separated by their times of flowering and appearance of the flowers. The Red Helleborine is a very rare species now known from only four sites in the Chilterns, Cotswolds and South Downs. Its flowering is sporadic and unpredictable, but when flowers do appear they show during June and July, and are a brilliant purple-pink,

rather long, narrow and unscented. They are longer than the leaf-like bracks, have pointed, spreading and hairy sepals with broad petals that bend inwards with an unspurred, whitish lip. The Violet Helleborine is a local species most frequent on the chalk of south-east England but extending as far north and west as the Welsh borders in Shropshire. It favours beech-wood on chalk, and flowers in August and September. These flowers are pale greenish-white inside and purplish-green outside, and are shorter than the leaf-like bracts at their base. The leaves are greyish above and heavily tinged with purple below and the plant prefers very dark situations. The Broad-leaved Helleborine, our most frequently observed species, is very variable. Flowers appear on a dense one-sided spike and are unscented, greenish-yellow or purplish, with pointed sepals and a heart-shaped tip to the unspurred lip. It occurs throughout the British Isles as far north as Scotland and is most often seen on calcareous soils where its flowers appear from July to September. The Narrow-leaved Helleborine occurs along the south coast in scattered localities and in Oxfordshire, the Welsh borders and the west coast from Cardigan to Sutherland where it is local and declining. It flowers in May, is pollinated by small bees, and is more slender and graceful than the Broad-leaved Helleborine with a less rigid stem which is much longer and narrower. Flowers are smaller, more spreading and widely open and are pure white with pointed sepals having an orange spot on the lip. Its preferred habitats are beech woodlands on chalk or limestone, where it is distinguished from the White Helleborine *C. damasconium* by its narrow, lanceolate leaves and its bracts being shorter than the ovary.

Ghost Orchid *Epipogium aphyllum* 12 cm

This extraordinary orchid has only been recorded appearing above ground a few times in the last hundred years. It is leafless, and has pale yellow stems, mauver above and thicker at the base. On these it has one to three hanging flowers, formed of palest yellow with a mauve lip bent back to touch the fat white spur which points upwards. It is overlooked because, lacking in chlorophyll, it is pallid and its varied colours camouflage it in the shady leaf litter of the chalky beech woodlands which it prefers. Flowers may appear any time between May and September and are pollinated by bumble bees.

Bird's-nest Orchid *Neottia nidus-avis* 30 cm

This orchid is almost entirely lacking in chlorophyll and is honey coloured all over. Its flowers have a rancid and sickly smell and are not spurred, the lowest often widely spaced down the stem giving the plant a loose resemblance to the broomrapes. This plant has an erect flower spike and large, two-lobed, hanging flowers. It is most common south and east of the line from The Wash to the Severn in the deep shade of beech-woods with humus rich soils. It flowers between May and July. Above the line it is scattered and rarer. Pollination is by small insects.

Greater Butterfly Orchid *Platanthera chlorantha* 50 cm

This species is most common in central and southern England, yet it is distributed throughout the British Isles, being only absent from the north-western islands. It occurs in wood and scrub on chalky soils where it flowers between May and July, being pollinated by night-flying moths. These moths are attracted by its vanilla scent, and use their slender tongues to extract nectar from a spur which may be three centimetres long. The elegant flowers are held in a rather pyramidal spike which is greenish-white with bright yellow pollenia. It has a single basal pair of elliptical, unspotted and unstalked stem leaves. Confusion is only possible with the Lesser Butterfly Orchid *P. bifolia* but this species is commonest in the north and is less frequent in woodland.

Fly Orchid *Ophrys insectifera* 50 cm

This species is locally distributed throughout England, as far north as Cumbria and north-east Yorkshire but is commonest in the south. Normally found in woods and scrub on chalk, it occasionally occurs on open downland. The flowers are very distinctive, bearing an obvious resemblance to an insect, and are pollinated by a male wasp which they mimic. It has shiny leaves, three green sepals, very antennae-like, narrow, dark brown petals, and a navy blue patch across the narrow, chocolate lip which is three lobed. Despite its characteristic appearance it can be hard to see in the dappled shade of the woodland floor.

Lords-and-ladies or Cuckoo-pint *Arum maculatum* 30 cm

This low hairless perennial has a large stalk, and dark green and bluntly arrow-shaped leaves often spotted with purple which emerge from the roots as early as January. The flower is a woodland favourite. It is held in a pale green hood whose lower bulbous part conceals the flowers. These are tiny, the male above the female in dense whorls around the base of a cylindrical, clubbed spadix, the visible part of which is a rich purple. Pollination is by owl midges which enter the floral chamber having been attracted by the heated spadix. These flowers appear in April and May and the fruit are conspicuous red poisonous berries which appear in July and August. The plant is distributed throughout the whole of the British Isles as far north as Scotland where it is common in woodlands.

FUNGI

Fly Agaric *Amanita muscaria* 8-20 cm

This species is unmistakable, having a cap up to 20 cm across, freckled with distinctive white pyramidal warts which may be washed off by rain leaving the cap smooth and the colour faded. This cap is supported by a stem up to 18 cm long, covered in shaggy remnants of its bulbous casing.

A bracket fungus on beech

It appears from late summer to late autumn, particularly in association with birch trees. This species is common and very poisonous.

Honey Fungus *Armillaria mellea* 3-10 cm
This species can be found in dense clusters on trunks and stumps of deciduous trees from summer to early winter. It is very common and has whitish to reddish brown stems supporting a cap measuring from 3-15 cm across which is very variable in shape and an ochre tawny to dark brown in colour. The centre of the cap is darkened to olive by small scales. The gills begin white and the whole cluster decays into a sticky chocolate slime after spring.

Porcelain Fungus
Oudemansiella mucida 2-8 cm
This species grows in large clusters high up on the trunks of beech. It is more easily observed on fallen trees. Here it appears in late summer to autumn where it is easily distinguished by its pale greyish to pearl white caps, which are semi-translucent and slimy. These are supported by a thin white stem which may be up to 10 cm long.

Beefsteak Fungus
Fistulina hepatica 10-25 cm
This fungus is common in late summer and autumn on the lower trunks of oak and chestnut. It is named because its mottled dark flesh is pink with lighter veining and has the appearance of raw meat. Its upper surface is moist, tacky and rough with rudimentary pores, especially towards the margins of the bracket. The whole appearance of the fungus is that of a tongue-shaped piece of meat.

Cep *Boletus edulis* 8-20 cm
This edible fungus is often seen for sale in continental markets. It is collected from summer to late autumn from all types of woodland, and identified by its smooth brown and initially dry cap. In time ·the cap becomes greasy and in wet weather polished, often being scarred by slug

damage. The thick stem may be up to 20 cm long and 7 cm in diameter and is a pallid white. The spores of this species are discharged from pores which with age become increasingly yellow.

Identifying all of the plants and fungi found in deciduous woodland is well beyond the scope of this book. Many species such as the familiar Bluebell *Hyacinthoides non-scripta*, Primrose *Primula vulgaris*, and Foxglove *Digitalis purpurea* have been excluded and reference to more specialized text is needed to identify the many more species of plants, and trees. These include Bugle *Ajuga reptans* the intricate blue flowers of which appear from May in wooded clearings; Lily-of-the-valley *Convallaria majalis*, which sometimes forms thick carpets over drier ash wood floors; Ivy *Hedera helix*, which is both ubiquitous and wide spreading; Herb Robert *Geranium robertianum*, the pink and very common annual; Herb Bennet *Geum urbanum*, the June flowering perennial; the pretty yellow Lesser Celandine *Ranunculus ficaria*; the shade tolerant Sanicle *Sanicula europaea*, which often grows in the deep shade of beech-woods; and a host of other easily identifiable species such as Bittersweet *Solanum dulcamara*, Black Bryony *Tamus communis*, Early-purple Orchid *Orchis mascula*, Goldilocks *Aster linosyris*, Oxlip *Primula elatior*, Snowdrop *Galanthus nivalis* and the unusual Purple Toothwort *Lathraea clandestina* and Mistletoe *Viscum album*. The identification of the ferns, fungi, lichens, liverworts and mosses is also complex and more specialized reference should be taken from the bibliography provided at the back.

INVERTEBRATES

Speckled Wood *Pararge aegeria* 4.5 cm
This species frequents woodland glades and pathways and shaded country lanes. It has a weak, flitting flight and sunspots in the shadow of overhanging trees are its typical habitat. Here it sits with its wings wide open sunning itself, showing its characteristic blackish-brown, ground colour wings which are marked with yellowish blotches and small black ringed eye spots. The female has more rounded wings and is slightly larger with lighter ground colour, but the markings resemble those of the male. The undersides are similar in both sexes. The adult lives between twelve and fourteen days and is on the wing from April onwards, into late June, second broods often appearing in August and are even on the wing as late as October in a dry summer. This species can be found commonly in small woods over much of southern England and Ireland and in less numbers in northern England, Wales and north-west Scotland.

Small Pearl-bordered Fritillary
Clossiana selene 4.2 cm
This species can be distinguished from the Pearl-bordered Fritillary with its wings closed. It has a row of light coloured spots across the middle of the underside of the hind-wing which in this species are all silver or all yellow, compared to the single silver spot of the Pearl-bordered. It frequents woodland glades and ridings, where it has rapid flight close to the ground fluttering then gliding, and seldom strays far from its colony in the wood. The colour of the upper sides of the wings is a rich golden brown marked and spotted with a similar pattern to those of the Pearl-bordered, the female being a darker insect. This species is widely distributed and locally common in many parts of Britain including Wales and Scotland.

Pearl-bordered Fritillary
Clossiana euphrosyne 4.6 cm
This species is a little larger than the Small Pearl-Bordered Fritillary, and like that species it has a row of spots across the middle of the underside of the hind-wing, but these are yellow except for the middle one which is a clear silver. Sexes can be distin-

guished by the female having darker markings and more rounded wings than the male, and the species has a rapid fluttering flight close to the ground, often gliding for short distances. It will bask with wings spread, but normally rests with wings closed and is most frequent in woods and coppices where there are open clearings where dog-violets are present. Now commonest in south and south-west England, it also occurs in Wales and Scotland and may be found as far north as Inverness.

High Brown Fritillary
Fabriciana adippe 5–6 cm
In dull, sunless weather this species will roost well hidden amongst the canopy of leaves but on sunny days it frequents woodland rides and clearings, where it is especially attracted to thistles and is notable for its swift and powerful flight. It has a few small red, silver-centred spots on the underside of its hind-wing between the silver wing-border and the central spots,

and this separates it from the downland species, the Dark Green Fritillary *Argynnis aglaia*. The butterfly emerges in mid-July and is on the wing for most of August although it is now the rarest of our larger fritillaries. Its range extends from southern England to the Lake District but it has disappeared from many of its former haunts.

Silver-washed Fritillary
Argynnis paphia 5.4–7 cm
This species is our largest fritillary and its powerful fluttering and direct gliding flight through woodland ridings and glades can be seen from June through to August. Feeding with their wings open, it is difficult to see the greenish coloured undersides of the hind-wings, which have the silver markings running across which gives the species its name. The uppersides of the wings show the typical fritillary black-spotted, bright orange and brown pattern. The female has a base colour of a tawny-olive with similar markings to the males. The washes of silver on the underwing are

Buff-tip on birch

Poplar Hawkmoth

what separates this fritillary from the others, which have clearly defined silver spots.

Heath Fritillary *Mellicta athalia* 4 cm
This is a species that is only found in woodland, favouring areas of recently cleared undergrowth where its cow-wheat foodplant can thrive. The butterfly emerges in late June and is on the wing for most of July. The male has a ground colour of a rich orange-brown marked with a pattern which forms the three transverse bands across the fore-wings. Hind-wings are similarly marked. Both wings have black borders and are edged with orange crescents. The female is a more tawny-brown and has lighter markings. On emerging these butterflies seem to congregate in open spaces in the wood and are easy to find at the end of the evening when they rest on grass heads, flower heads or rushes. In contrast to the larger fritillaries the flight is weak and fluttery. The species is unfortunately now very local in Britain

and is most frequent in a small part of east Kent. Small numbers may also occur in Essex, Devon and Cornwall.

Purple Emperor *Apatura iris* 7.5 cm
This butterfly emerges in July and is on the wing during the first half of August, now unfortunately being uncommon and found only locally in wooded areas in southern England, extending as far north as Oxfordshire and Northamptonshire. Here it frequents large woodlands and forests, where it soars with a powerful gliding flight around the topmost branches of standard trees, usually oak. Purple Emperors, however, may be more easily seen feeding from dung and carrion on woodland rides or attracted to brightly coloured cars in car-parks. The adults are a stunning insect, having a ground colour of plain chocolate brown covered with a brilliant purple sheen on both fore- and hind-wings. There is a broken white band on the forewings and a continuous one on the hind wings, which are decorated with a

rust red ring spot. Females are identical but lack the iridescent purple. On the underside the white markings are similar but the ground colour is a mixture of red-brown and buff to dark brown.

White Admiral *Limenitis camilla* 6.5 cm

This species can be seen on the wing from mid-July to mid-August, when it frequents clearings along sunny ridings and is noted for its strong but elegant gliding motion over the Bramble blossom and Honey-suckle on which it feeds. Highly distinctive from above, it is primarily black with a white stripe crossing both fore- and hind-wings. The underside ground colour is rusty brown with three rows of black spots set in the marginal band with the white bands of the upper side repeated on the underside. Sexes are superficially similar, the females always being a slightly larger insect with a paler ground colour. The adults rest with their wings wide open, and live for fourteen to eighteen days. Mainly a southern species it can be found more sparingly as far north as the Midlands, but is absent from Ireland and Scotland.

Purple Hairstreak
Quercusia quercus 3.2 cm
Brown Hairstreak *Thecla betulae* 3.2 cm
Black Hairstreak *Strymonidia pruni* 3 cm

The Purple Hairstreak is perhaps most commonly seen dancing in a weak flutter-ing flight high up around the branch of its favourite oak tree. If one can be seen hav-ing descended, it basks with its wings wide open showing the males greyish-black colouring with a purplish sheen and black borders to its wings. Females are velvety black with brilliant iridescent purple patches on the basal half of the fore-wings. Both sexes carry a short tail on the hind-wing which may often be absent due to it breaking off. This butterfly fre-quents woodland glades and the outskirts of wooded country and is on the wing dur-ing July and August. The Brown Hairstreak is more frequently seen feeding on Bramble blossom and scattered about

Blackthorn thickets where it settles fre-quently with wings closed. The male's upper wings are brownish-black with a small streak next to a light creamy-yellow patch near the centre of the fore-wing. The margin of the hind-wing is slightly scal-loped, whilst the female is a rich, dark brown with wide tawny-orange bands across the fore-wing and a dark streak similar to the male. It is, however, the undersides which are characteristic, being a bright orange-brown ground colour marked with a small black streak and a wedge-shaped brown bar, edged with white across the fore-wing. In flight these underwings flash distinctively and are con-spicuous when the butterfly is at rest, as are the body and legs which are white. The Black Hairstreak also always rests with its wings closed, but is more familiarly seen on flowers of wild privet. Males' upper wings are dark brown with a series of three orange crescent marks on the hind-wings which have a short black tail with white tip. The underside is of a golden brown with a curved line of white dots running across the fore-wings and continuing on the hind-wings. This line forms a conspicuous W in the White-letter Hairstreak *Strymonidia W-album*. Sexes are similar and fly from the end of June into July, when they frequent the margins of woods and clearings where Blackthorn grows. This species is unfortunately one of our rarer indigenous butterflies and is limited to a few woods in Huntingdonshire, Northamptonshire and Oxfordshire, whilst the Brown Hairstreak is now common only in southern England and a small area of western Ireland. The Purple Hairstreak is widespread in the woodlands of southern England and extends into Wales and Scotland.

Hornet *Vespa crabro* 3 cm

This insect is easily distinguished from the rest of our social wasp species by its relatively enormous size, and much more ochreish rather than canary yellow colour-ing. The thorax is marked with a dark chestnut brown top and the insect has its

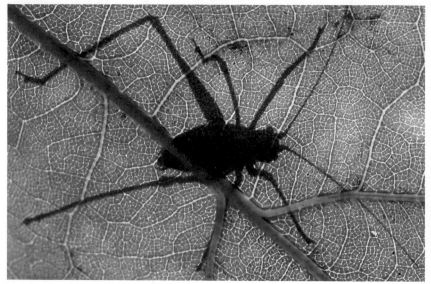

The shadow of an Oak Cricket

wasp black markings replaced by reddish-tan, which also tinges the ochrish legs. For its nest the Hornet prefers hollow trees, upright or fallen, where it may use old woodpecker holes or natural cavities. Here they are most frequently seen in late summer hovering around the entrance. Hunting insects are frequently encountered in sunny woodland glades where their deep humming and powerful direct flight make them difficult to observe but nonetheless characteristic.

Longhorn Beetle
Rhagium bifasciatum 1.4–2 cm

This is a typical long-horned beetle and one of 70 of our native species. The adults are faintly pubescent and show a great deal of variability in the elytral pattern, having two well marked yellowish bands which make the species distinct. The edge of the elytra is commonly a reddish-chestnut brown with a dark central stripe. The upper parts of the legs are a dark browny-black and lower parts a fleshy yellow. These beetles are most commonly found in

decaying wood and stumps in which their larvae may also be found. They are common in most parts of the British Isles and occur in the greatest numbers in woodlands that have many rotting stumps – their favourite haunt.

Cardinal Beetles
Pyrochroa coccinea 2 cm,
P. serraticornis 1.2 cm,
Schizotus pectinicornis 0.8 cm

These three species are so named because of their brilliantly coloured scarlet elytra. They are frequently found under the bark of old tree stumps, but in summer in sunny weather they can be seen feeding on woodland flowers. The head is strongly constricted behind the eyes, and in *coccinea* and *pectinicornis* it is black, whilst in *serraticornis* it is red. Size can be used to distinguish the three species, as can the pectinacous antenna which are most apparent in *pectinicornis*, the smallest of the three species, which may also have a black thoracic spot. All are widespread in the British Isles.

Common Buzzard

Stag Beetle *Lucanus cervus* 2-5 cm
This species showes strong sexual dimorphism, indeed the much smaller females, lacking the exaggerated mandibles of the male, may be confused with the Lesser Stag Beetle *Dorcus parallelipipedus*. Male Stag Beetles are the largest of our native beetles and belong to a family more typically habiting the tropics and renowned for their mandibular extensions. It is thus easily recognized by its large size and pitch to dark brown elytra which is darker in the females. It is most frequently seen late in the evening when it may be attracted by artificial lights and its presence can be noted by the distinctive buzzing and its wafting and wavering flight. The huge larvae have powerful jaws for biting through their deadwood home which they may inhabit for three years or more. This species is decreasing and more common in southern England particularly south of the Thames.

Woodland supports and provides the habitat for many thousands of insect species.

Those conspicuously absent from this text include the moths Lepidoptera, including the large and beautiful hawkmoths Sphingidae, the mainly cryptic Noctuidae, and the many Geometrid and Torticid species whose larvae feed on trees. The trueflies Diptera, the gall wasp Cynipidae, the social wasps Vespinae, the wood wasps Siricidae, the bees, the huge family of beetles Coleoptera and the ants are all well represented in woodlands as are the slugs and snails, and the arthropods, centipedes, millipedes, etc. A more specialist book list is provided in the bibliography and reference should be made to these for more information and identification.

VERTEBRATES

Buzzard *Buteo buteo* 51-56 cm
Honey Buzzard *Pernis apivorus* 51-59 cm
Buzzards are easily identified by their characteristic compact flight silhouette, having broad wings, large evenly barred rounded tails and very short necks. Adults

are very variable in colouration ranging from dark brown through to very pale or white individuals. In spring particularly the species can be seen soaring for hours on broad motionless wings with the tips of the primaries uncurved and the tail widely spread. Wings are held straight and slightly raised into a shallow V. The short neck gives a very blunt appearance compared to that of the Honey Buzzard which has a longer neck projecting forward from the more narrow base of the broad wings. In this species the tail appears much longer and has a dark terminal band and only two narrower bands near the base. Again the plumage is very variable in colour, ranging from dark brown above and lighter brown below to an almost completely brown bird. This species soars and hovers less than the Buzzard, its wings droop very slightly with upturned tips when soaring, and it has deeper wingbeats when flying. Both species make large conspicuous nests in deciduous trees, the Honey Buzzard showing a preference for those on the edge of a ride. In the British Isles the Honey Buzzard is now a very rare bird, occurring at only a few locations in the south. The Buzzard, however, occurs sparsely in Ireland but regularly down the western side of Scotland, England and Wales, a distribution influenced by the pesticide pollution problem.

Goshawk *Accipiter gentilis* 48–61 cm
Sparrowhawk *Accipiter nisus* 28–38 cm
These species can be distinguished from other birds of prey by their combination of short rounded wings, long tail, and rapid wing beats between long glides in flight. In both species the female is much larger than the male. Female sparrowhawks have blackish-brown upper parts with a white stripe above and behind eye, and whitish underparts closely barred with grey, whilst males have slatey-grey upper parts with rufus cheeks and a whitish spot on their nape. The underparts have fine red-brown bars. The buzzard-sized Goshawk's colouration resembles that of the female Sparrowhawk but it has sturdier legs and broad-based wings which may look pointed except when soaring. Immatures resemble females. Despite the vast difference in size, in the field scale can be the difficulty in separating these species unless they are visible at the same time. However, Goshawks have a particularly conspicuous white undertail covert, often appearing like a large white flag in flight, and their tails appear relatively shorter and more rounded than Sparrowhawks and are fanned when soaring. Both species make a rapid 'Kek – Kek' call, and are best observed in spring when they have a conspicuous territorial and mating display over their woodlands. As a result of the pesticide pollution problem of the 1950s Sparrowhawks show a more westerly distribution in the British Isles. Goshawks are a recent re-colonization/re-introduction and are becoming more widespread, although they are now more common in the north of England and Scotland.

Woodcock *Scolopax rusticola* 35 cm
This unusual wader is quite unmistakable but it shows an incredible crypsis when it roosts on the leafy floor. Its underparts are finely barred and buffish and it has transverse black bars across the top of its head and neck. Its beak is long and straight and its legs shortish for such a bulky body. Because of its crepuscular and nocturnal activity it is rarely seen in the woodlands other than in flight. Here, however, it is conspicuous, particularly during summer when it performs its 'roding' flights. These are a slow display flight along regular routes above trees performed at dawn and dusk. Males have a soft croaking 'Oorrrtorrt' followed by a high sneezing 'Tsiwick.' Other flight is usually rapid and dodging and the bird looks stout and neckless. They frequent damp woods and coppices where they lie up during the day and seldom move before dusk. Woodcock are widely but locally distributed in the British Isles and are found in all suitable localities. Most British and Irish woodcock are

believed to be sedentary, but in winter an influx from Scandinavia, Russia and Germany occurs.

Tawny Owl *Strix aluco* 38 cm
Long-eared Owl *Asio otus* 36 cm

Both of these species are strictly nocturnal but can be readily separated. The Tawny Owl has a heavier build, black eyes, and no ear tufts, whilst the long-eared in flight appears to have longer wings and tail, and its wings are less fingered. The Long-eared also often glides with wings in a shallow V. At rest it has conspicuous ear tufts and bright orange eyes set in a more angular head, atop a more slender body. The tawny varies in colour from a warm brown to greyish, with bold dark streaks, whilst the Long-eared has streaked upper parts of mottled buff and grey-brown and paler underparts. The call too can be used to separate the species. The Long-eared emits a long sighing *'OO – OO – OO'*, with a much more moaning cry than the Tawny Owl which makes a shrill *'Ke – wick'*, and has a familiar *'Hoo – Hoo – Hoo'* song. At the end of the summer the young of Long-eared Owl are conspicuously noisy, making a call akin to the squeaking of a rusty gate. Choice of habitat too is different, the Long-eared being less common in deciduous woodland whilst Tawny Owls prefer mature mixed woodland. Tawny Owls are widely distributed across the British Isles but are rarer in parts of northern Scotland and entirely absent from Ireland, whilst Long-eared owls are a lot less common and show an even distribution over the rest of the British Isles, including Ireland.

Green Woodpecker *Picus viridis* 32 cm
Great Spotted Wodpecker
Dendrocopos major 23 cm
Lesser Spotted Woodpecker
Dendrocopos minor 14.5 cm

In the British Isles we have only three species of woodpecker, all of which are easily separated in the field. The Green is the largest, with dull green upper parts, pale green underparts and a bright crimson crown. In flight it shows a conspicuous yellow rump and lower back and this flight is deeply undulating with long wing closures between each upward bound. A similar flight pattern is seen in the Great Spotted Woodpecker which is considerably smaller than the Green and again considerably larger than the Lesser Spotted Woodpecker. It is distinguished from the Lesser Spotted by its black back with large white shoulder patches and crimson undertail coverts. An unbroken black bar runs across the cheek and the underparts are white with a sharply defined red patch below the tail. Males have a crimson nape patch and immatures of both sexes have entirely crimson crowns. Lesser Spotted Woodpeckers are the smallest European woodpecker and are distinguished from all the other pied woodpeckers by their sparrow size, closely barred back with white underparts and absence of any red on the tail coverts. Forehead, cheeks and underparts are whitish with a few streaks and the male has a dull red crown (the females crown is whitish). The behaviour of the three species also does not overlap. The Lesser Spotted spends most of its time in the upper branches fluttering amongst twigs. The Great Spotted seldom feeds on the ground whilst the Green Woodpecker spends long periods on the ground, often at ants' nests. Green Woodpeckers seldom drum whilst Great Spotted drum rapidly on dead branches but with a slower frequency than Lesser Spotted. The call of the Green is a loud ringing laugh whilst the Great Spotted makes a sharp *'Tchick'* or *'Kik'*, which is louder and more frequent than the very similar *'Tchick'* made by the Lesser Spotted. The Great and Lesser Spotted are more woodland birds than the Green Woodpecker, which may be found in more open parks and farmlands with scattered trees. The Green Woodpecker is absent from Ireland and becomes less frequent as one passes through northern England to Scotland where it is absent from all of the isles and the north and most highland regions. The Greater Spotted extends further into Scotland and is equally widespread in Wales and England, as is the Lesser Spotted, the least frequent of all of the species, which has a more southerly distribution.

Redstart *Phoenicurus phoenicurus* 14 cm
The Redstart is a summer visitor to Britain from its winter quarters in West Africa. Both sexes are exceptionally conspicuous due to their constantly flicking rusty red tail and rusty rump. The male has a boldly marked black face and throat, with a white forehead and slate-grey upperparts. His chest is an orangey-chestnut brown. The female is a duller greyish-brown above and buffish below. They are most often encountered in open woodland and in clearings, where in spring courtship chases can be seen in and out of the scattered trees. The song is a pleasing jingle of hurried notes, rather like a Robin, which fades into a feeble trill. The most familiarly heard call is a liquid *'Wheet'* resembling a sharper Willow Warbler and also a clear *'Tooick'*. In the British Isles the Redstart is largely absent from Ireland and shows a westerly distribution throughout Scotland, England and Wales. Despite this it still occurs in all of the English counties.

Wood Warbler
Phylloscopus sibilatrix 12.5 cm
Willow Warbler
Phylloscopus trochilus 11 cm
Chiffchaff *Phylloscopus collybita* 11 cm
These species are collectively known as the leaf warblers because of their habit of appearing in the leafy canopy and because of their greenish or olive appearance. The Wood Warbler is conspicuously larger than both the Chiffchaff and Willow Warbler and can be distinguished by its brightly contrasted yellowish-green upper parts and sulphur yellow throat and breast. It also has a bold stripe above the eye and a conspicuous display in spring. It makes a slowly repeated *'Stip'* which accelerates into a crescendo of a grasshopper like trill *'Stip-Stip-Stip-Stip-Stip-Stip-shreeeeeee.'*

This it performs high in the canopy with fluttering wings. Another song is a high piping *'Piu'* repeated five to twenty times. Otherwise its behaviour is like the Chiffchaff but it does not flick its wings, although they often hang loosely. Willow Warblers are the most abundant summer visitor to northern Europe and may be confused with the Chiffchaff, except for their distinctive song which is a musical cadenza, beginning quietly and becoming clearer and more deliberate and descending to a distinctive flourish *'Soeet – Sooeetto.'* The call is also distinct being a *'Hooeet'* compared to the soft *'Hweet'* and subdued *'Tsif – tsiff – Tsiff'* of the Chiffchaff. The Chiffchaff is more arboreal than the Willow Warbler, which looks slightly greener above and yellower below, less dumpy and longer winged than the dingier and compact Chiffchaff. Chiffchaffs have a blackish bill and legs which are pale in the Willow Warbler. Their upper parts are olive brown, underparts buffish white very faintly tinged with yellow and both wings and tail constantly flick when feeding. The Wood Warbler is largely absent from Ireland and shows a westerly distribution in Scotland, Wales and England where it favours woodland which has a good canopy, little secondary growth and sparse ground vegetation. Chiffchaffs occur widely in Ireland and England, becoming less frequent as one goes north in Scotland, whilst Willow Warblers show an ubiquitous distribution, being only less common in the northern and western isles. All three species are summer visitors, but some Chiffchaffs overwinter. Despite their arboreal habits all three species are ground nesting.

Pied Flycatcher
Ficedula hypoleuca 12.5 cm
Spotted Flycatcher
Muscicapa striata 14 cm
These species are most frequently seen perched upright on vantage points in the canopy. From here they make short sallies and erratic chases after passing insects.

Pied Flycatchers have readily separable sexes. The male in breeding finery has a black head and upper parts and a white forehead and underparts. Also conspicuous is a white wing patch and white sides of an otherwise black tail. The female is an olive brown above and buffish white below and has similar paler wing patches. Its call is a metallic *'Whit'* and a persistent *'Tic'* or *'Wheetic'*. Its song is a Redstart-like trill spaced with two up and down notes, and its behaviour differs from the Spotted Flycatcher because after a feeding sally it seldom returns to the same perch and often it will feed on the ground. Spotted Flycatchers have pale brown upper parts, a spotted chin and a delicately streaked white breast. Sexes are inseparable and their wings and tails are often flicked. Their voice is a thin grating *'Tzee'* and a rapid *'Tzee – tuc'* and the song is a sharp and quick series of notes. Spotted Flycatchers make a nest like a Chaffinch's against tree-trunks or behind creepers where they lay up to five brownish-marked eggs in late May. Pied Flycatchers nest in holes in trees or nest-boxes if provided and can be locally very common whilst showing a distinct south-westerly distribution in the British Isles. They are absent from Ireland and are most frequently encountered in Wales where the damp, old oak woodland provides an ideal habitat. Spotted Flycatchers are ubiquitous and occur over all the British Isles with the lowest density populations on the north and north-western isles.

Treecreeper *Certhia familiaris* 13 cm
Nuthatch *Sitta europaea* 17 cm

A small brown tree-climbing bird, the Treecreeper is easily distinguished from woodpeckers and nuthatches by its small size, thin down-curved bill and distinctive behaviour. It climbs up trees in short bursts with its stiff tail pressed against the bark searching for insects in the cracks and crevices. It is brown above, with various darker and paler streaks, and off-white below. The tail is long and brown with pointed feathers, and the wings are short and rounded with a conspicuous pale crescent wing bar in flight. This flight is deeply undulating, rather feeble and moth-like. The eyes are large for such a small bird and are hidden by an unusually large eyebrow which gives the bird a somewhat bad-tempered expression, again emphasized by the long bold eye-stripe. Nuthatches on the other hand are dove grey above, white on the throat and a rich cinnamon tinged brown on the underbelly. They also have a conspicuous black eye-stripe running from the base of their short straight bill through their eye and on to the nape of their neck. In flight they are similarly broad winged and have conspicuous black carpal patches. Unlike the normal behaviour of the Treecreeper, which ascends trees, the Nuthatch may climb in any direction including downwards. The voice of the Nuthatch is also very distinctive, a ringing *'Chwit, Chwit, Chwit'* or a repeated *'Tsit'*, whilst the song is a repeated and a very loud *'Tui'* and a long trilling *'chi-chi-chi-chi'*. Nuthatches prefer Beech, oak, Sweet Chestnut and Hornbeam, and whilst the Treecreeper is resident and found over all of the British Isles, the Nuthatch is absent from Ireland, Scotland and parts of northern England.

Jay *Garrulus glandarius* 35 cm

These unmistakable birds can be heard making a raucous *'Skaraaaak'* amid other various harsh notes, clickings and mewings, especially in summer in their family groups. However, when nesting they can be very quiet and inconspicuous. That, however, their plumage certainly is not. They have a white rump contrasting with a black tail, a bold white patch on the wings, and blue and barred iridescent blue and black barred wing coverts. They also have an erectile crown streaked brown and white and pale blue eyes. The remainder of the body is a pastel pinkish-brown. Flight is heavy and often undulating and birds are often seen in parties, especially in autumn when quite large groups may

May Bluebells and Jay

frequent oak-woods searching for acorns. Jays occur over much of southern, central and northern England and the Scottish lowlands; they are, however, absent from many parts of the Scottish highlands and islands. In Ireland they show a distinct easterly distribution.

The tits Paridae, finches Fringillidae, and many warbler species from the family Sylviidae, join the thrushes Turdidae in being conspicuously absent from this text. Their groups are of course well represented in woodland by a number of species such as the Blue Tit *Parus caeruleus*, Great Tit *P. major*, Willow Tit *P. montanus*, Marsh Tit *P. palustris*, Long-tailed Tit *Aegithalos caudatus*, the Chaffinch *Fringilla coelebs*, Bullfinch *Pyrmula pyrmula*, Hawfinch *Coccothraustes coccothraustes*, the Blackcap *Sylvia atricapilla*, Garden Warbler *S. borin*, the Icterine Warbler *Hippolais icterina*, Melodious Warbler *H. polyglotta* and the Robin *Erithacus rubecula*, Blackbird *Turdus*

merula and Song Thrush *T. philomelos*. The Woodpigeon *Columba palumbus*, Stock Dove *C. oenas* and Pheasant *Phasianus colchicus* are frequently encountered and easily identified.

Hedgehog *Erinaceus europaeus* 56 cm
These entirely nocturnal, woodland insectivores are quite unmistakable because of their spiny pelage. The underbelly has a sparse and coarse fur and males are usually bigger than females. They are easily located by searching with a torch, especially in wet grassy areas where they appear very noisy. However, their own response to any noise is to roll into the characteristic ball entirely protecting their legs, head and other extremities. Hibernation begins in October and ends in April. Grassy woodland edges are the preferred habitat and here they can be found snuffling and snorting when searching for their food and often emit loud pig-like squeals when alarmed. Smell and hearing are acute. Hedgehogs are found all over Britain and Ireland.

Red Squirrel *Sciurus vulgaris* 37–40 cm
Grey Squirrel
Sciurus carolinensis 46–49 cm

The Red Squirrel is easily distinguished from the grey by its deep brown to rich chestnut pelage, the Grey being greyish with yellowy-brown along its back. The Red also has a shorter, more rounded facial expression and ear tufts. The Greys are twice as heavy, appearing much more sturdy than the lithe Reds. Sexes of both species are indistinguishable in the field. The presence of both species is easily noted by scattered scales and stripped cores of pine cones, split shells or husks of beechmast or Hazel nuts and their untidy leafy dreys. In Britain, it is now habitat which is the easiest way of separating these species, since the Red is confined to coniferous woodlands in much of its range, whilst the Grey is most abundant in mixed mature hardwood. Both species are quite vocal, Red Squirrels uttering a chuckling call and explosive whirring sounds, while Grey Squirrels scold with a *'chuck-charrey'* call, which is often quite lengthy, and a low *'tuck – tuck.'* The distribution of Red Squirrels in Britain is now 'patchy' but shows a distinct northern bias, being found in Scotland, northern England, North Wales and much of southern Ireland. Isolated pockets do occur, such as the Isle of Wight, areas of Cornwall and the north Norfolk coast. Greys, however, can be found over much of southern England, up through the Midlands, East Anglia, the whole of Wales, into the north Midlands and over a large area of the Scottish lowlands. Interestingly, one of the major areas of southern England where they are not found is the Isle of Wight.

Wood Mouse
Apodemus sylvaticus 15–17 cm
Yellow-necked Mouse
Apodemus flavicollis 22–25 cm

Wood Mice are, in a manner of speaking, typical mice having large, prominent ears and eyes and long nearly hairless tails. The coat is a sandy colour with some adults showing much brighter yellow on the flanks and a darker brown appearance on the centre of the back. This form of the Wood Mouse is separated from the Yellow-necked Mouse by the small size or absence of the chest spot seen in the Yellow-necked. Here a yellow collar appears to be consistently well developed and the upper coat is a rather richer reddish-brown. Both species are predominantly nocturnal with dusk and dawn peaks of activity in winter and their locomotion is rapid, either scurrying or leaping, unless cautiously investigating when slow deliberate steps are taken. In the field they may occasionally be discovered by torchlight by their distinct jerky rustlings of the undergrowth as they progress across the dry leafy floor. Food is mainly seedlings, nuts, fruits, buds and small arthropods, and in winter the major items are tree seeds. Fungi, moss, bark and galls are also consumed. Preferred habitat is mixed woodland with Bracken and Bramble yet they are common in all woodland types, and also in hedgerows and fields. Yellow-necked Mice are often found with Wood Mice and yet are usually less common than that species. In Europe Yellow-necked Mice are more truly woodland animals whilst Wood Mice occupy field and scrub. In Britain the Wood Mouse is widespread on all but some small islands and large areas of open moorland whilst the Yellow-necked Mouse is restricted to southern England and Wales and absent from large areas within that range, i.e. from most of the south west and the Midlands.

Common Dormouse
Muscardinus avellanarius 15 cm
Fat Dormouse *Glis glis* 32 cm

Scale and colouration easily distinguish these two species. The Fat Dormouse is about double the size of the Common Dormouse and is a uniform greyish-brown except for dark rings around the eyes and slightly darker stripes on the outside of its legs. It is white below. The Common Dormouse has upper parts and tail of a very uniform orangey-brown and an underside of pale buff with pure white on its throat. Its tail is well furred but narrow, whilst that of the Fat Dormouse is fluffy and flattened in the horizontal plane. The Fat Dormouse frequents mature deciduous woodland but also orchards and gardens and unlike the Common it does not require a dense scrub layer. It is a very agile climber, spending most of its life in the tree canopy, and is entirely nocturnal. Nests are built in a fork close to the trunk and it hibernates from October to April. The Common Dormouse is best located by searching for its nests, and these are most apparent when set above ground in the cleft of a sapling. About 15 cm in diameter, they are commonly made entirely of Honeysuckle bark, and there is no clearly defined entrance hole. The Common is also strictly nocturnal, and hibernation lasts from October to April. It is generally quiet but shrill squeaking noises have been recorded. Not indigenous to Britain, the Fat Dormouse was introduced at Tring in Hertfordshire where it spread to a limited extent in the Chiltern Hills, whereas the Common Dormouse, which is confined to England and Wales, is widespread but local in suitable habitats in southern Britain. It favours deciduous woodland with secondary growth and scrub, especially hazel, Sweet Chestnut and beech, and it occurs frequently in coppices and species-rich hedgerows.

Polecat *Mustela putorius* 45–52 cm
Polecats are distinguished from mink by the creamy wool over much of their body, and from escaped polecat ferrets by their much darker appearance and more restricted white facial band. They have a typical mustelid build, and the two white patches between the eyes and ears elongate towards the jaw as the animal grows older. In autumn the patches elongate across the forehead, sometimes joining completely but are more often separated by a grizzled area. Droppings are a useful guide to the species presence. When fresh they are usually black, full of fur and fragments of small bones, up to 70 mm long and 5 mm wide. They are often twisted with tapering ends. Polecats are mainly active at night when they make a variety of sounds ranging from chattering to a sharp scream when frightened or enraged. Hearing and smell are the senses largely used in hunting. This species is distinguished from weasels by its much larger size and from stoats by its generally dark colouration, as opposed to pale red. Distribution in Britain was formerly widespread, but now it is restricted to all of the Welsh counties except Anglesey. It also occurs in Herefordshire, Gloucestershire and Shropshire as a result of expansion in the 1950s.

Badger *Meles meles* 80–100 cm
These nocturnal omnivores are quite unmistakable in the field, having a white head with conspicuous black stripe down either side running through the eye, their wedge-shaped bodies appearing grey from a distance. Their legs are short and well clawed for powerful digging, also giving distinct footprints which are usually visible in the sand outside their setts. Males have broader heads, thicker necks and rather narrow pointed white tails. Female badgers are considerably sleeker and have a much broader and greyer tail. They are generally silent but the cubs make a high-pitched whinnying when tiny and female badgers can often make a bird-like barking call. Setts are easily distinguished from fox earths by the diameter of their burrows which must be at least 20 cm and by the large heaps of soil outside the hole. Senses of smell and hearing are very acute but eyesight seems at times exceptionally poor. Cubs are born from mid-January to mid-March, and usually of one to four in number, and they remain below ground for about eight weeks before emerging in April. In Britain badgers occur in every county, being commonest in the southwest and rarest in East Anglia. They are, however, absent from most of the islands off Britain, excluding Anglesey and the Isle of Wight.

Red Deer *Cervus elaphus* 122 cm
Fallow Deer *Cervus dama* 95 cm
Roe Deer *Capreolus capreolus* 66 cm

Measurements are shoulder heights
These three species are easily separated in the field

	RED DEER	FALLOW DEER	ROE DEER
Summer coat colour	Red–brown	Reddish-fawn spotted with white	Reddish-fawn
Antler types	Elongate, tined	Elongate, palmate	Short, pronged
Antlers shed/regrown	March/July	May/August	November/April
Rump pattern	Tailed, plain, pale	Tailed with black crescents and stripe over white	Tail-less, plain, cream
Rutting period	September/October	October/November	Summer

Roe Deer, the smallest European deer, also have shorter and higher heads with short, pronged antlers and long necks, whilst Red Deer, the largest, has elongate, heavily tined antlers, swept backwards from the top of a longer head and shorter neck. Fallow Deer have palmate antlers and less conspicuous ears than Roe. Roe also have a large-eyed appearance.

Red Deer are the only large red to brown deer without spots in Britain. Summer coat, usually predominantly red, sometimes dark brown or yellow, in winter changes to brown, but may be almost black. The belly is off-white or grey. They have a well developed social structure with a segregation of the sexes outside the rutting season. Woodland groups are seldom more than family parties, except during the rut. The Reds' alarm call is a short, sharp bark, or series of barks by hinds. Stags roar during the rut which occurs from the end of September to mid October. Usually only a single calf is born from the third week of May to the second week in October. Their senses of sight, smell and hearing are acute so if you want to get close, patience and care are needed.

In Fallow Deer many colour varieties occur, ranging from nearly white to black, but the most common summer coat is a reddish-fawn with white spots along the flank and back, and a black vertebral stripe extending right along the back. Antlers on one- and two-year-old males may form small knobs or spikes. Unlike any of our other deer species palmation of antlers begins to occur in the third year. During the day Fallow Deer lie up in vegetation moving at dusk to the rides and open areas to feed. Older stags are mainly nocturnal and are rarely seen except at the height of a rut when they often appear oblivious to man's presence. Sexes remain separate for most of the year, but young males will stay with the females for the first twenty months. They are usually silent but, when rutting, males make a repeated deep loud belching noise, and females, when in danger, give a short, sharp bark sometimes repeated two to three times.

Roe deer are the smallest of these three deer species and appear almost tail-less, although females have an anal tuft of hair. (Rump pattern is a useful identification feature for these three deer species. Red Deer have a pale rump region and tail, whilst Fallow Deer have a longer tail lined with a thin black stripe and convergent crescents around the white rump cushion. Roe have an almost imperceptible white tail on a small white rump patch with no black.) The rest of the Roe Deer coat varies from sandy to bright reddish-brown with paler underparts in summer and from greyish-brown to almost black in winter.

Antlers seldom exceed 30 cm in length and show no palmations, being pronged and upright. Males hold territories from April to August,.and although they are generally solitary they may congregate to form herds in winter. Two fawns are born between mid-May to mid-June.

Although absent from Wales, the Roe Deer is increasing its range in England, central southern England, parts of Norfolk and Northumberland and all but the north of Scotland and some of its isles have this species. Fallow have a more southerly distribution with introduced pockets around the rest of the country, and Red Deer have a more northern bias, although they are still found in English woodlands, particularly in East Anglia, and parts of the Midlands.

Sika Deer *Cervus nippon* 75 cm
Chinese Water Deer
Hydropotes inermis 60 cm
Muntjac *Muntiacus reevesi* 50 cm
Measurements are shoulder heights
Rump pattern is also useful for separating these three species from each other and

Sika from Fallow Deer. Sika share the black crescent around a white rump patch with Fallow Deer but lack the central black stripe. Muntjac have longer and broader tails, lightly marked with a paler brown, and Chinese Water Deer have tails which are almost absent in males, and thinly lined with black in females. Sika are a medium sized deer whose coat is generally chestnut red with straw to white spots in summer. In winter it is a greyish-brown with no or very faint spots, similar in pattern to those of Fallow Deer. Its body is altogether stockier than Fallow with antlers that are not palmated and lacking the number of tines found in Red Deer, reaching only six to eight points in mature stags. A nasal whine can be very characteristic, producing the sound of a gate hung on rusty hinges swinging in the wind, becoming more whistle-like and like a hoarse shriek towards the end of the rut. This species prefers deciduous woodland on damp or poorly drained soils with a dense undergrowth of Blackthorn, hazel, Bramble or other shrubs. An introduced species in

A Muntjac buck hiding in a thicket

England, feral herds are established in Dorset, Hampshire and west Yorkshire. In Scotland they are found in Argyll, Caithness, Invernesshire, Peebleshire and Sutherland, and in Ireland they are established in County Dublin, Kerry and Wicklow. They also occur on the island of Lundy in the Bristol Channel.

Chinese Water Deer have only been established outside Woburn in the last forty years, so they are limited to an area of Bedfordshire in England. Slightly larger than a Muntjac, with a paler sandy colour, this species never has antlers but can be distinguished by its large broad ears and protruding tusks. Little is known of their behaviour in Britain, other than they are active at dawn and dusk, and have a whistling call during the rut which takes place in December. Fawns are born in late May and early June, with a litter that is unusually large for deer, with up to five being born at once.

Muntjac are the smallest deer to be found in the British Isles. Their coat is a chestnut colour and males may be distinguished from females by their stockier, thicker necks and females having more orange on heads, shoulders, and antler pedicles, which are also notably large. Antlers are cast in May and June and are regrown by October to November. This species likes very dense, mixed or deciduous woodland, and its social structure is based on a family unit, males and females remaining together throughout the year. Nocturnal, they can occasionally be seen in the evening, and may emit single barks every four or five seconds for continuing periods of up to forty-five minutes. The Muntjac, like water deer, was introduced in Bedfordshire in 1900 and since the 1950s has spread through south-east England.

Many other small mammals may be found in deciduous and mixed British woodlands, depending on the ground flora. Pigmy Shrews *Sorex minutus* and Common Shrews *S. araneus* occur widely, whilst Rabbits *Oryctolagus cuniculus* and

A decaying beech

Brown Rats *Rattus norvegicus*, although not prominently woodland species, can be found in most of the woodlands in the British Isles. Bank Voles *Clethrionomys glareolus* are also encountered, as are the predators such as the Stoat *Mustela erminea*, Weasel *M. nivalus* and the Red Fox *Vulpes vulpes*. Joining these species are a host of bat fauna, many of which are difficult to identify if they are not in the hand but in the field. The most common are Common Pipistrelles *Pipistrellus pipistrellus* and the Noctule *Nyctalus noctula* which can be seen flying after dusk. The Noctule is a large swift-size bat flying on broad wings, whilst the Pipistrelle is a tiny bat which flits in tight curves around the edges of trees, snatching small, flying insects. Other bat species to frequent such areas include Natterer's Bat *Myotus nattereri*, Daubenton's Bat *M. daubentoni* and Common Long-eared Bats *Plecotus auritus*.

BRITISH WOODLAND NATURE RESERVES: ENGLAND

This list is not intended to be a guide to all woodland reserves, but only some of the best. All map references are Ordnance Survey 6 figure, except in the case of large areas where 4 figure references are given. All abbreviations are spelt out in full on their first use.

Avon

Ebbor Gorge. ST 525488. 46ha. Nature Conservancy Council.
This water cut gorge in the Mendip plateau is topped with ash woodland and some limestone scrub. The lower woodland is oak, ash and coppiced hazel which dates from the Bronze Age, whilst the former species date from the mid-nineteenth century. The under storey is of smaller ash and oak with Wych Elm, Field Maple, common Whitebeam, Small-leaved Lime and Hawthorn. In spring the carpet of Bluebells dissolves into Dog's Mercury and a host of other common woodland plants such as Yellow archangel, Bugle, Early Dog-violet and Wood Sorrel. The rarer species include Broad-leaved Helleborine, Greater Butterfly Orchid and Purple Gromwell whilst a bevy of ferns exist in the damper areas including the rare Tunbridge Filmyfern. Most common birds occur along with over 30 species of butterfly. These include White-letter Hairstreak and High Brown fritillary, both uncommon, and one of the reasons why this woodland is worth a visit.
Others: Avon Gorge (ST 553731), Cheddar Woods (permit only, S.T.N.C.), Great Breach Wood (permit only, S.T.N.C.), Thurlbear Wood (permit only, S.T.N.C.).

LEFT **A fungal parade of parasols**
RIGHT **An early morning web**

APPENDICES

Bedfordshire and Huntingdonshire

Monks Wood. Permit only. 156ha.
Nature Conservancy Council.
One of the most famous pieces of woodland in Britain, its history is very well known. The woodland is of oak standards above coppiced stools of ash, Field Maple, and hazel. This is now managed on a rotation to give a full range of such woodland types and, in conjunction with some adjacent scrub and ponds, yields a superb species diversity. Wild Service Tree, Dogwood, dense thickets of Hawthorn and Buckthorn occur over Cowslips and Wild Primroses, which cross to give the False Oxlip. Crested Cow-wheat grows on the woodland edges with Violet Helleborine in the shade, along with a host of commoner species such as Common Twayblade, Birds-nest and Greater Butterfly Orchid, Herb Paris, Common Star of Bethlehem, Musk Mallow and Small Teasel. All three species of hairstreak butterflies occur along with a host of moths and over 1,000 different species of beetle and the wood is important as a key site for several of these. A typical range of birds occurs and some of the coppiced stands are very favourable for the nightingale.

Others: Aversley Wood (TL 160817), Flitwick Moor (TL 046354), Holme Fen (permit only, N.C.C.), Kings Wood (TL 037393), Waresley Wood (permit only, Bedfordshire & Huntingdonshire Wildlife Trust).

Berkshire

Windsor Great Park. SU 953735. 6,000ha. Crown Estate Commissioners.
These ancient oaks were planted from Elizabethan times onwards, to supply timber for the navy, but other gnarled and holed specimens are reputed to be even older. This age is shared with very few standing forests and this has survived because of its former standing as a royal hunting forest. These ancient trees hold on their decaying limbs and stumps a tremendous range of fungi, including three rarer species of *Boletus*. Over 2,000 species of beetle have been recorded along with two fly species which only occur here and may fall prey to a good range of woodland birds including a range of warblers, all three woodpeckers, Redstarts, Nightjar and Woodlark. Red, Fallow, Roe and Muntjac skulk about and five species of skipper butterfly flit over a diverse range of woodland plants.

Others: Moor Copse (permit only, Berks., Bucks & Oxfordshire Naturalists' Trust, B.B.O.N.T.).

Buckinghamshire

Church Wood. SU 973873. 14ha. Royal Society for the Protection of Birds.
Eighty species of birds have been recorded, over forty of which breed in this mixed woodland of birch, oak, beech, ash and conifers. Brambles spread over the ground between clumps of Hawthorn and over 200 species of plants have been noted including Green Helleborine, Solomon's Seal, Wood Spurge and Butcher's Broom. Holly Blues, White-letter Hairstreaks and White Admiral butterflies occur with the familiar range of woodland insects and mammals.

Others: Chalkdell Wood (SP 900012), Chesham Bow Wood (SP 960003), Tenterden Spinney (SU 967995).

Cambridgeshire

Hayley Wood. TL 295536. 49ha.
Cambridgeshire and Isle of Ely Naturalists' Trust (Cambient) Reserve.
A coppice of hazel, Field Maple and ash occurs under oak standards on a rich clay base with an under storey of Hawthorn and Midland Hawthorn. A combination of habitats of differing woodland age and coppicing gives a good range of habitat which supports about 280 flowering plants (Saw

Wort, Crested Cow-wheat, Herb Paris, Wood Millet). Eighty mosses and liver-worts, including *Nowellia curvifolia*, and 70 species of fungi are also found. Typical woodland birds, like woodpeckers, Tree-creepers and in winter flocks of tits, flit about in this woodland with 700 years of recorded history.

Others: Aversley Wood (TL 158815), Knapwell Wood (permit only, Cambient Reserve), Fordham Wood (permit only, Cambient Reserve), Papworth Wood (permit only, Cambient Reserve), Wicken Fen (TL 563705).

Cheshire

Warburtons Wood. Permit only. 3ha. Cheshire Conservation Trust (C.C.T.).
Damp banks swamped with horsetails, hogweeds, buttercups and Bramble occur here with drier areas supporting Bettony, milkwort, Quaking Grass with the rarer Dyer's Greenweed and Lady's-mantle. Honeysuckle, wild rose and guelder-rose grow over the ancient Wild Service Trees and Small-leaved Limes. Elsewhere, oak, hazel, Hawthorn, Rowan, Wild cherry, Elder and Holly stand above carpets of Ramsons, Bluebells, Wood Anemone, Wood Sorrel, Red Campion, Dog Violets and Primroses. Indeed this reserve is mainly of botanical interest although it supports the expected woodland birds.

Others: Dibbinsdale (SJ 345827), Risley Moss (SJ 663921), Styal Country Park (SJ 835830), Thornton Wood (permit only, C.C.T.).

Cornwall

This county is not famed for its woodland and no large and outstanding reserves exist. The following are all small but worthy of specific visits. The **Hayman** (permit only. 1.8ha. Cornwall Trust for Nature Conservation (C.T.N.C.)) has oak and Sweet Chestnut over Bluebells, Enchanter's Nightshade, Sanicle and an array of ferns. **Pelyn Woods** (permit only. 40.4ha. C.T.N.C.) have Sweet Chestnut with beech and sycamore, with a typical range of woodland life. Similar to this is **Pendarves Wood** (permit only. 24ha. C.T.N.C.), whilst **Peters Wood** (SX 113910. 10ha. C.T.N.C.) is a steep valley woodland which cuts back from the coast and is notable for its range of species typical of acid woodland including Daubenton's, Common Long-eared and Leisler's bats. Further woodlands include **Antony Wood** (SX 401547), **Benskins Wood** (SX 409539) and **Shute Wood** (SW 742522).

Cumbria

Roundsea Wood and Mosses.
SD 335825 and 351802. 7ha. Nature Conservancy Council.
Geological formations make this woodland vary from acidic to alkaline, over slates and limestone respectively. On the slate, oak, birch, Rowan and Holly stand above an under storey of hazel with Bracken and Purple Moor-grass while over the limestone ash, oak, Small-leaved Lime, Yew and Crab Apple cover giant bellflower, Columbine, Herb Paris, Bird's-nest Orchid and Toothwort. Other Cumbrian woods of note include **Dorothy Farren Spring Wood** (permit only. Cumbria Trust for Nature Conservation, C.T.N.C.), **Dubbs Moss** (permit only. C.T.N.C.), which holds a fine array of mosses and ferns, **Grubbins Wood** (permit only. C.T.N.C.) which is an old, limestone, coppiced wood (permit only. C.T.N.C.) and **Park Wood** (permit only. N.C.C.).

Derbyshire

Ogston Woodlands. Permit only. 32ha. Derbyshire Naturalist Trust (D.N.T.).
Access is by permit only to this piece of

primary woodland which shows a great range of types of broad-leaved woodland. Oak, Rowan and Holly are joined by ash, beech, Silver Birch, Wych Elm and alder and the range of ground cover is equally varied. Wood Sorrel and Anemone, Climbing corydalis, Creeping Jenny, Wood Horsetail, Wood Speedwell and Wood Stitchwort grow beneath the Bracken, and ferns and mosses cover the ragged stream. A good range of birds can be seen from a well placed hide and these include Treecreepers, Nuthatchs and woodpeckers along with Sparrowhawks and Tawny Owls representing the carnivores.

Others: Brockholes Wood (permit only, D.N.T.), Elvaston Castle Country Park Nature Trail (SK 413332), Ladybower Wood (permit only, D.N.T.), Spring Wood (permit only, D.N.T.).

Devon

This county abounds with useful pieces of woodland worth exploring and contains at least thirty reserves owned by the Woodland Trust. Other important tracts can be found in the **Welcombe and Marsland Valleys** (permit only off paths. R.S.N.C.), **Dart Valley** (SX 672733–704704. Dartmoor National Park Authority (D.N.P.A.) – Devon Trust for Nature Conservation (D.T.N.C.) and **Dartmoor National Park** (D.N.P.A.). Other than these, **Black Tor Copse** (SX 567890). Nature Conservancy Council) is interesting for its stunted oaks, lichens, mosses, ferns and Ring Ouzels as is the more famous **Wistman's Wood** (SX 612772. N.C.C.) which grows in the extremes of rain, wind and bouldered ground. Less harsh, and more typical woods can be found at **Blackadon** (SX 712732. D.T.N.C.) where oak grows over Billberry; **Bovey Valley Woodlands** (SX 789801. N.C.C.) which is rich in mosses, liverworts and ferns; **Dendles Wood** (permit only. N.C.C.) which has Pied Flycatcher, Redstarts and Buzzards in 300-year-old beech; **Lady's Wood** (SX 687

591. D.T.N.C.) which has Dormice; and the extremely varied **Shaptor and Furzeleigh Woods** (SX 819797, Woodland Trust) with its Dwarf Oaks, coppiced beech and invading birch.

Dorset

Bracketts Coppice. ST 517072. 22ha. Dorset Nature Trust.
In a county more famed for its heaths and coastline this reserve is worthy of attention being a wet woodland of oak standards over old hazel coppice. Ground cover is scant but woodland grasses, ferns, primrose, Bugle, violet and spreads of Ivy and Enchanters Nightshade cover the floor as do spectacular carpets of Pendulous Sedge. **Fifehead Wood** (ST 778218. Woodland Trust), **Horse Close Wood** (ST 715045. Woodland Trust) which has the locally uncommon meadow saffron, and **Stonecrop Wood** (ST 988955. Woodland Trust) are other small reserves with specific points of interest.

Durham, Cleveland and Tyne and Wear

Castle Eden Dene. NZ 410387. 200ha. Peterlee Development Corporation.
This is probably the least spoilt of the valleys running down to the North Sea. The sometimes steep sides of the dene are covered in a rich variety of woodland comprising oak, ash, Yew, beech and Sycamore growing with introduced blocks of Sweet Chestnut, Horse Chestnut and Hornbeam. Scattered Wild Cherry, Rowan, alder, Holly, hazel, Hawthorn and elder also occur. This diverse tree fauna gives rise to the accompanying range of smaller plants from the Bluebells, anemones, primroses, ramsons, and Dog's Mercury to the lesser common round-Leaved Wintergreen, Lily-of-the-valley, Giant Bellflower and Bloody Cranesbill. Nuthatches are at their northern limit here where they occur with most other typical woodland birds

joined in winter by Dippers, Bramblings, Waxwing and Siskins, whilst at the bottom of the wood waders occur as the river meets the sea. Here too a good range of maritime plants can be found.

Others: Collier Wood Nature Trail (NZ 129364), Hawthorn Dene (permit only, Durham Council Conservation Trust), Rosa shafto (NZ 245350), Thornley Wood (NZ 185612).

Essex

Essex has some fine woodland reserves including **Blakes Wood** (TL 775064) with its Hornbeam and Sweet Chestnut; **Hatfield Forest Country Park** (TL 546199) a coppice with oak standards and many interesting features; **Marks Hill** (TQ 684874); **Norsley Wood** (TQ 692957); **Shadwell Wood** (permit only. Essex Naturalists' Trust, E.N.T.) which has a fine floral range; and **Weeleyhall Wood** (permit only. E.N.T.) which has some interesting insect fauna in its old oaks. However the county holds one of the largest remaining ancient forest – only 25 km from the centre of London stands **Epping Forest**. This ex-royal hunting forest is dominated by long overgrown beech pollards, with other stands of oak and glades of Hawthorn. In places the dense shade of the beeches reduces the ground flora to almost nothing and this reduces some of the insect fauna, notably the butterflies. The beetles make up for this a little with 1,400 species recorded. Woodland birds are typical with good sites for Hawfinch and all three woodpeckers. The Badgers and Fallow Deer have gone, but Muntjac occur regularly but inconspicuously.

Others: Hales Wood (permit only, N.C.C.O, Norsey Wood (TQ 692957), Scrubs Wood (TL 787058), Westhouse Wood (permit only, E.N.T.), West Wood (permit only, E.N.T.).

Gloucestershire

Frithwood. SO 877086. 22ha.
Gloucestershire Trust for Nature Conservation (G.T.N.C.).
The Cotswolds hold some fine high beech woodlands, one of which is Frithwood. Because the wood is on a ridge, light enters horizontally and allows the development of a dense under storey. The ground cover is varied including Sanicle, Woodruff, Enchanter's Nightshade, Wood Mellick, Spurge Laurel and Broad-leaved Helleborine. Such ground cover provides for a diverse invertebrate fauna, which is particularly rich in snail species. Another such beech woodland occurs at the **Cotswood Common** and **Beechwoods** (SO 894131. N.C.C.), which holds Common Wintergreen, Narrow-lipped and Green Helleborine, Bird's-nest orchid and Yellow Bird's-nest.

Others: Buckhole Wood (SO 874131), Collin Park Wood (permit only, G.T.N.C.), Lassington Wood (SO 803203), Littleton Wood (permit only, Avon Wildlife Trust), Magshead (SO 606080), Silkwood (permit only, G.T.N.C.).

Greater London

Perivale Wood. Permit only. 11ha.
Selborne Society Reserve.
This mainly oak woodland with patches of hazel, ash and Wild Service Tree is one of the oldest nature reserves in Britain (1904). A fair range of plant species occurs including good stands of Bluebells, Red Campion and Wood Millet. Typical woodland birds can be seen. Bear in mind that Epping Forest is only a tube ride away.

Others: Hainault Forest Country Park, Hampstead Heath, Harfield Place, Nunhead Cemetry, Old Park Wood (permit only, Hertfordshire & Middlesex Trust for Nature Conservation), Selsdon Wood, Sydenham Hill Wood, Upper Wood.

Hampshire

This county is very rich in woodland reserves, but is dominated by those found within the boundaries of the **New Forest** (37,500ha. Forestry Commission). Half of this area is afforested and it is the largest spread of lowland woodland in north-western Europe, trees 200–300 years old, mainly beech and oak but also Sweet Chestnut, ash and Sycamore. Grazing by the ponies often reduces the ground flora to nothing, although rarities such as Narrow-leaved Lungwort, Coral Necklace and many fungi and lichens can be found. The forest is superb for larger mammals, daylight emerging Badgers can still be found in places, a small number of Red Deer, a few hundred Roe and a great number of Fallow can be seen along with Sika Deer. Woodland bird species abound with good numbers of Hawfinch, Wood Warbler, Lesser Spotted Woodpecker, Buzzard and Sparrowhawks. Insects are equally well represented with a beetle fauna unequalled elsewhere, Britain's only cicada and an unfortunately declining butterfly fauna. All in all this area is the woodland to visit with many car parks, and paths into the woodlands.

Others: Ashford Chase (SU 729266), Crab Wood (SU 436398), Old Winchester Hill (SU 647210), Roydon Woods (permit only, Hampshire & Isle of Wight Naturalists' Trust), Selborne Hill (SU 73337), Upper Hamble Country Park (SU 490114), Wealden Edge Hangers (SU 729266).

Hereford and Worcester

Wyre Forest. SO 759766. 300ha. Nature Conservancy Council.

This forest has an extremely wide variety of habitats with many different forms of native woodland, high oak forest, rich mixed woodlands in valleys and on clay soils. These are mainly birch over Bilberry, Bracken, Heather, Wood Sage and Lily-of-the-valley. In other places Hawthorn, hazel and Rowan cover roses, Wood Mellick, Wood Spurge and Wood Sorrel. Less common ground plant species include Columbine, Narrow-leaved Helleborine, Bloody Cranesbill and Intermediate Wintergreen. A fine range of moths occur with some typical woodland butterflies and a number of interesting wasps, spiders and other invertebrates including our only land-living caddis larvae. The wooded stream attracts Kingfisher, Grey Wagtail and Dipper whilst Woodcock, the three woodpeckers, Redstarts, Nuthatches and the expected warblers flit about the woodlands. All in all this is one of the finest woodland reserves in the U.K.

Others: Aileshurst Coppice (permit only, Worcestershire Nature Conservation Trust, W.N.C.T.), Brockhampton Woodland Walks (SO 893543), Doward Group (permit only, Herefordshire and Radnorshire Nature Trust, H.R.N.T.), Holywell Dingle (permit only, H.R.N.T.), Hunthorse Woodland (permit only, W.N.C.T.), Nunnery Wood Country Park (SO 877543), Ravenshill Wood (SO 739539).

Hertfordshire

This county holds a number of woodlands worth a local visit. **Balls Wood** (permit only, Hertfordshire and Middlesex Trust for Nature Conservation, H.M.T.N.C.) has Goldilocks Buttercup, Slender St. John's wort, Wood Small Reed, White Admiral butterfly and Fallow and Muntjac deer. **Hopkyn's Wood** (permit only, H.M.T.N.C. has oak over Hornbeam over Primrose and Ramsons. Dormice and Badgers are resident. **Northern Great Wood Country Park** (TL 283038), noted for its Nightingales, is a beech, oak and Hornbeam woodland. **Wormley Wood** (TL 317062 is Sessile Oak over Hornbeam coppice and attracts the usual range of woodland bird fauna and common plant flora.

Others: Fordham Wood (TL 337398), Fox Covert (TL 337398), Pryors Wood (permit only, H.M.T.N.C.).

Kent

Yocklett's Bank. TR 125467. 25ha. Kent Trust for Nature Conservation (K.T.N.C.).
Kent has a number of fine chalk woodlands but this particular wood is perhaps the most famous for its population of Lady Orchids. This is the prime site for this species but also Common Spotted, Early Purple, Fly, Pyramidal and Greater Butterfly Orchids occur with a host of other woodland plants such as Yellow Archangel, Ramsons, Enchanter's Nightshade and Sanicle. The tree species are oak over coppiced Sycamore on the clay soils and ash, beech and Hornbeam over coppiced hazel on the chalk.

Others: Branchley Wood (TQ 648418), Blean Wood (TR 118611), Burnt Oak Wood (permit only, K.T.N.C.), Ellenden Wood (TR 109625), Hunstead Wood (permit only, K.T.N.C.), Kiln Wood (TQ 888515), Stockbury Hill Wood (permit only, K.T.N.C.).

Lancashire

Not a county renowned for its woodlands the following are listed for local visiting. **Alkrington Woods Nature Trail** (SD 864053), which is beech woodland with a good range of woodland birds; **Astley Park Nature Trail** (permit only, Cheshire Conservation Trust, C.C.T.), which is good for fungi and birch moss, is a birch and Bracken woodland; whilst **Brooley's Coverts** (permits only, C.C.T.) holds a good range of trees and birds; **Compstall** (permit only C.C.T.) has a good range of birds boosted by a river; **Redscar** and **Tunbridge Woods** (permit only, Lancashire Trust for Nature Conservation) shares this avian bias, whilst **Roddles-**

worth Nature Trail (SP 665215) has a range of ferns to supplement its Redstarts, Wood Warblers and Woodcocks.

Leicestershire and Rutland

Swithland Woods. SK 538129. 58ha. Bradgate Park Trust.
High forest oak over birch and Foxgloves grows over much of the reserve while on the wetter part an alder-ashwood covers Willowherb, valerian, Nettle, campion and Bugle. Under the oaks Basil Thyme with wood-rush, Wood Sorrel, Bluebell, Yellow Pimpernel and Common Cow-wheat flourish. Less common plants include Betony, Adders Tongue and Sawwort. As part of the ancient Charnwood Forest this is worth a visit to see typical woodland fauna and a diverse flora.

Others: Ambion Wood (permit only, Leicestershire & Rutland Trust for Nature Conservation, L.R.T.N.C.), Great Fenny Wood (permit only, L.R.T.N.C.), Great Merrille Wood (permit only, L.R.T.N.C.), Pickworth Great Wood (permit only, L.R.T.N.C.).

Lincolnshire and South Humberside

Much of the forests have been cleared from this county, however a few sites remain as reserves worthy of a visit. **Bardney Forest** (permit only, F.C.) is a fragment of a once great spread of ash and Small-leaved Lime and its varied ground cover attracts a range of insects and birds. **Birds Wood** (permit only, Lincolnshire & S. Humberside Trust for Nature Conservation, L.S.H.T.N.C.) is aptly named for the 70 species recorded here along with 12 species of butterfly. **Rigsby Wood** (TF 420761) is oak and ash and has Early Purple Orchid, Woodruff and Woodcock as a winter visitor. **Tortoiseshell Wood** (permit only, L.S.H.T.N.C.) has ash and oak over hazel, Field Maple and Wild Service Tree. Yellow Archangel, Early Purple and

103

Greater Butterfly Orchid occur as do Fallow Deer and Nightingales.

Others: Dole Wood (permit only, L.S.H.T.N.C.), Friskney Decoy Wood (permit only, L.S.H.T.N.C.), Hoplands Wood (permit only, L.S.H.T.N.C.).

Norfolk

A county more renowned for its coastal sites and moors, it nevertheless has several woodland reserves of note. **Felbrigg Great Wood** (TG 204403) has some ancient beech woodlands with associated bird fauna; **Thurlsford Wood** (permit only, Norfolk Naturalists' Trust, N.N.T.) comprises oak standards over hazel, with ash, beech and birch in places. Bluebell, Wood Anenome and Wood Sorrell grow on the floor. **Wayland Wood** (permit only, N.N.T.) is another coppice with standard sorrel type woodland, this time oak over hazel on a very damp floor where Yellow Star of Bethlehem and Early Purple Orchid occur, with Bluebells and Primroses. Rather unique is **Methal Old Thorn** (TG 172004) which is a reserve with a single tree, namely the oldest Hawthorn in the UK reputed to have been planted in the reign of King John.

Others: Bure Marshes (permit only, N.C.C.), East Wretham Heath (TL 914886), Sandringham Country Park (TF 689287), Strumpshaw Fen (TG 342067), Uptron Fen (permit only, N.N.T.). Many of these include wet fen woodland or carr.

Northamptonshire

Short Wood. Permit only. 24.8ha. Northamptonshire Trust for Nature Conservation (N.T.N.C.).

A remnant of an ancient forest, this is said to be the best Bluebell wood in Northamptonshire set under high ash forest with oak and hazel. Of particular interest are the high stooled coppiced elm, the

locally rare Wood Speedwell, Early Purple, Greater Butterfly and Bird's-nest Orchid and Broad-leaved and Violet helleborines. Fallow Deer can also be seen.

Others: Castor Highlands (TF 118023), Delf Spinney (permit only, N.T.N.C.), Clapthorn Cowspasture (permit only, N.T.N.C.), Kings Wood (SP 864874), Newbottle Spinney (SP 517364), Salcey Forest (permit only, N.T.N.C., B.B.O.N.T. and F.C.), Thorpewood (TL 160986).

Northumberland

Goose's Nest Bluebell Bank (NY 980852) has one of the county's finest bluebell spreads, and **Grasslees Burn Wood** (permit only, Countryside Commission, C.C. – Northumberland Wildlife Trust, N.W.T.) has one of the largest alder-woods in the country with a damp and mossy floor and Pied Flycatcher, Wood Warbler and Redstart as avian visitors. **Kidland Woods** (permit only, N.W.T.) are upland and moor-edge woodlands which contain the uncommon Chickweed Wintergreen. The lower woods contain a rich variety of trees and birds such as Pied Flycatcher, Redstart, Wood Warbler and Grey Wagtail. **Plessey Wood Country Park** (NZ 238800) has Red Squirrel, Roe Deer, Dipper and Tawny Owl. **Priestclose Wood** (NZ 107628), an oak and birch wood, has a varied bird life and a typical woodland ground flora.

Others: Arnold (NU 255197), Barrow Burn wood (permit only, C.C. – N.W.T.), Long Nanny Wood (permit only, N.W.T.), River Tyne Gravels (permit only, N.W.T.), Slacks Plantation (permit only, N.W.T.), Tony's Parch (permit only, N.W.T.).

Nottinghamshire

A remnant of **Sherwood Forest** (SK 627677) with its old Pendunculate an

Sessile Oaks, is an important reserve for beetles. **Sellers Wood** (SK 523455) holds some secondary woodland blending in from a heath. Birch, ash, elm, Hawthorn and Hazel grow over wood Mellick and Giant Bellflower and the woods provide a range of ecotypes with many of the typical species associated with each. Ash and Pendunculate Oaks predominate in the ancient **Treswell Wood** (permit only, Nottinghamshire Trust for Nature Conservation, N.T.N.C.) where a great range of other trees also occur in this old coppice. New management should see an improvement in the ground flora which currently supports Wild Angelica, Self-heal, Bluebell and Primrose.

Others: Fox Covert Plantation (permit only, N.T.N.C.), Hannah Park Wood (SK 590773), Oldmoor Wood (SK 497428).

Oxfordshire

Foxholes (permit only, B.B.O.N.T.) has a belt of woodland consisting of oak, ash, hazel and Blackthorn over Meadowsweet and Common Spotted Orchids, whilst Shotover Country Park (SP 561063) has a series of nature trails through an old hunting forest where Fallow Deer and Muntjac still dwell in the coppice and standard woodland. Varied woodland types can be found at **Warbury** (SU 720880) where a similarly large range of ground cover occurs including Columbine, Green Helleborine, Herb Paris and Solomon's Seal. Woodland mammals are all well represented, Badger, Fox, Stoat, Weasel, Fallow Deer and Muntjac, as are the birds (Wood Warbler, Sparrowhawk, Woodcock) and insects which include a good range of moths. **Wynchwood Forest** (permit only, N.C.C.) has several small ponds and is an important site for lichens.

Others: Blenheim Park (SP 442168), Chinnor Hill (SP 766002), Lawknor Copse (permit only, B.B.O.N.T.), Vale Wood (SP 237040).

Shropshire

Edge Wood. Permit only. 10ha.
Shropshire Trust for Nature Conservation (S.T.N.C.).
Here some areas have survived the planting of conifers, and oak and ash flourish with a range of other tree species over Bluebells, Wood Anemone and Dog's Mercury, Herb Paris, Sanicle, Woodruff, Wood Sorrel and Wood Spurge, and Early Dog-violet contrasting with some grassland species in this mixed aged coppice which supports six tit and warbler species each. Well worth a local visit.

Others: Bushmoor Coppice (permit only, S.T.N.C.), Corbet Wood Trail (SJ 525238), Earl's Hill (SJ 409048), Ercall Wood (SJ 646103), Hope Valley Woodland (SJ 350018), Wallow Coppice (permit only, S.T.N.C.).

Staffordshire

A few remnants of the ancient oaks remain in the county, the rest having been used as charcoal for industry. **Burnt Wood** (permit only, Staffordshire Nature Conservation Trust, S.N.C.T.) is one such place which has moss covered timbers and old stumps and which supports a wide range of insects including Small Pearl-bordered Fritillary and some locally uncommon moths. **Coombes Valley** (SK 005530) has the High Brown Fritillary amongst 24 butterfly species, 500 moth and over 1,200 beetles under the shade of its mainly oak woodland. **Hem Heath Wood** (SJ 885412) has some 34 species of tree with a host of underflora, including Twayblade and Broad-leaved Helleborine. **Jackson's Coppice** (permit only, S.N.C.T.) is in a small shallow valley with an exposure of sandstone covered in mosses, lichens and ferns, beneath an oak and beech wood. Pied Flycatchers abound at **Rough Knipe** (SK 009534) along with other birds.

Others: Chance Wood (permit only, W.N.C.T.), George Hayes Wood (permit only,

S.N.C.T.), Hemley Wood (SO 869916), Parrott's Dumble (permit only, S.N.C.T.), School Lane Wood (permit only, S.N.C.T.), Swineholes Wood (permit only, S.N.C.T.).

Suffolk

Bradfield Wood. TL 935581. 64.4ha. Suffolk Trust for Nature Conservation (S.T.N.C.).

These managed woods have the finest range of plants in East Anglia and give an insight into the appearance of woodlands of yesteryear. The rides too are unchanged and teem with insect, bird and plant life. Forty-two native shrubs have been found with over 350 flowering plants and the ensuing wealth of insect and bird-life. The latter includes a range of warblers along with Woodcock, the Woodpeckers and Tawny Owls. Roe, Fallow and Red deer occur along with Weasel, Stoat and Fox. All in all this is an extraordinary living remnant of woodland as it used to be and as such is worthy of a visit.

Others: Armstrongs Wood (TL 965638), Groton Wood (permit only, S.T.N.C.), Porter's Wood (TM 263493), Wolves Wood (TM 054436).

Surrey

Surrey has a number of small woodlands worthy of exploration. **Bagmore Common** (SU 926423, Surrey Trust for Nature Conservation, S.T.N.C.) is an acid woodland of birch and pine which holds over twenty-three species of butterfly including White Admiral and Purple Emperor, whilst **Nower Woods** (permit only, S.T.N.C.) is noted for its show of spring flowers, particularly Bluebells. **Ripszam's Wood** (permit only, S.T.N.C.) is particularly renowned for its butterflies, including White Admiral, Purple Emperor, Dark Green, Silver-washed and Small Pearl-bordered Fritillaries. These flit over plants such as

Common Centaury and Broad-leaved Helleborine which flourish in this oak and ash, with hazel, coppice which is now being actively restored. **Vann Lake** (permit only, S.T.N.C.) is renowned for its exceptional variety of fungi which includes over 560 species, one of which was unknown to science before its discovery here in 1973. To complement this, over 100 bird species have been recorded including Nightingale and all three woodpeckers. The wood includes Wild Service Tree, making it part of an ancient woodland, with an underflora of Bluebell, Primrose, Common Cow-wheat and several orchids.

Others: Boxhill Country Park (TQ 179513), Cucknells Wood (permit only, S.T.N.C.), Headley Warren (permit only, S.T.N.C.), Staffhurst Wood (TQ 412483).

Sussex

Sussex has a number of extraordinary woodlands worthy of visit. **Ashdown Forest** (TQ 432324) is an area of high weald woodland which was once a hunting forest. This extremely varied woodland holds populations of Fallow Deer, Badger, Fox, Stoat and Weasel, along with many species of woodland birds. Butterflies include Pearl-bordered, Small Pearl-bordered and Silver-washed Fritillaries. **Fore Wood** (TQ 756128) is a primary woodland site, unaltered by any management for many years. Half of the reserve is Sweet Chestnut coppice, the other half oak and birch. Hawthorn coppice is also in evidence and the show of flowers is particularly good in early spring. These include Primrose, Woodruff, Woodspurge, Wood Sorrel and Early Purple, and Common Spotted Orchids, Common Twayblade and Broad-leaved Helleborines. Birds include six tit species, all three woodpeckers, Nuthatch, Treecreeper, Tawny Owl and Hawfinch. **The Menns** (TQ 024236) has areas of high beech forest with little ground flora.

Other areas have oak and beech with a more open canopy, and under storey of Holly, Yew and hazel and these support ground floras of Wood Anemone, Bluebell, and Bugle. The high forest supports good populations of woodland birds, all three woodpeckers, many warblers and Sparrowhawks. Butterflies include White Admiral and Purple Emperor. Roe Deer are common whilst Fallow Deer and Muntjac may be seen occasionally. Parts of the reserve are famed for their fungal interest. **Nap Wood** (permit only, Sussex Trust for Nature Conservation, S.T.N.C.) consists of spaced trees over bracken, often invaded by birch with a carpet of Bluebells in spring. Other tree species include Crab Apple, Hawthorn, Holly and Wild Cherry with a ground flora of Ramsons, Yellow Archangel and Pendulous Sedge. Mammals include Fox and Badger, with a bird fauna including Redstart and Wood Warbler. **Woods Mill** (TQ 218137) is a small reserve with much of interest. It is an old coppice with ash, beech, Field Maple, Hawthorn, Holly and Wild Service Tree growing over Wood Anemone, Bluebell, Primrose, Wood Spurge, Wood Millet, and Dog Wood. Less common plants include Male Fern and Heart's Tongue Fern. A typical range of woodland bird occurs.

Others: Ebernoe Common (SU 976278), Flatroppers Wood (TQ 862229), Guestling Wood (TQ 863144), Mallydams Wood (TQ 857122), Powdermill Wood (permit only, S.T.N.C.), Saint Leonard's Forest (TQ 208299), Selwyn's Wood (TQ 552205), West Dean Woods (permit only, S.T.N.C.).

Warwickshire and West Midlands

This area is rather poorly wooded, however some small woodland reserves exist worthy of a local visit. **Clower's Wood** (permit only, Warwickshire Nature Conservation Trust, Wa.Na.C.T.) is composed of two woodlands, one a mainly even-aged oak over birch, Holly, Rowan, and Buckthorn, the other mature oak and beech drained by a small stream. Beneath this the ground flora is Wood Sorrel, Buckler Fern, Common Cow-wheat, and Lesser Spearwort. Both parts are noted for their mosses and fungi and contain some fine spreads of Lily-of-the-valley. A typical range of woodland birds and mammals occur, including over fifty locally uncommon species of moth. **Crackley Wood Nature Trail** (SP 287737) contains a fine showing of spring flowers such as Wood Anemone and Bluebell as well as a typical range of flora and fauna. **Ham Dingle Nature Trail** (SO 913828) has the usual range of woodland birds along with typical mosses and fungi in this oak woodland. Oak with birch over Holly comprises **Sutton Park** (SP 103963), which has little ground flora away from the woodland clearings where Bramble, Willow Herb, Bracken and Heath Bedstraw grow. **Tilehill Wood** (SP 279790) is an oak-hazel woodland, which despite heavy urbanization includes Wood Anemone, Bluebell and Wood Sorrel along with a typical range of bird and insect species. Oak over old coppice comprises **Wappenbury Wood** (permit only, Wa.Na.C.T.) which also contains ash, birch, Holly and Aspen. Thirty-seven species of woodland butterfly have been recorded here along with Woodlark, Tree Pipit, and Nightingale.

Others: Earl's Wood Moat House (permit only, Wa.Na.C.T.), Hart's Hill Hayes country Park (SP 315945), Roughwood Nature Trail (SJ 094010), Saltwell's Wood (SO 934874), Sandwell Valley Nature Trails (SP 017914), Tocil Wood (permit only, Wa.Na.C.T.), Welcoombe Hills Nature Trail (SP 205564).

Wiltshire

Blackmore Copse (permit only, Wiltshire Trust for Nature Conservation, W.T.N.C.) is a fine example of mixed woodland. Oak with a hazel under storey, it has a ground flora of Greater Bird's-foot Trefoil, Bugle, Meadowsweet, Yellow Pimpernel and Ragged Robin, along with more typical woodland species, such as violets, Primrose, Woodruff and Wood Spurge. Dormouse and Roe Deer occur here with a typical range of woodland birds. However pride of place goes to the wood's butterflies, which include White Admiral, Purple Hairstreak and Silver-washed Fritillary, along with Purple Emperor. **Colerne Park** and **Monk's Wood** (ST 835725) is a fine example of old coppiced oak and ash woodland which has interesting plants such as Solomon's Seal, Angular Solomon's Seal, and Lily-of-the-valley amongst its ground flora. **Ouster's Coppice** (permit only, W.T.N.C.) is an ash over oak and hazel woodland which has fine showings of Wild Daffodil and Bluebell in spring, with a variety of typical woodland mammals and birds including Wood Warbler. **Red Lodge Wood** (permit only, W.T.N.C.) is a relict of Bradon Forest being an oak over hazel, birch and Hornbeam wood. It supports Wood Anenome, Bluebell and Primrose with less common plants such as Broad-leaved Helleborine amongst its ground flora. Butterflies include White Admiral and Purple Hairstreak. **Savernake Forest** (SU 225667) is a fine spread of ancient woodland which was once a royal hunting forest. The conifers, beech, oak, ash, Rowan and Sycamore form a varied woodland structure with a rather limited ground flora. Around the rides Wood Avens, Enchanter's Nightshade, Dog's Mercury, Wood Spurge and Wood Sorrel grow, and typical woodland birds such as Sparrowhawk, Green Woodpecker and Nuthatch can be found along with Fallow, Red, Roe and Muntjac deer. Another remnant of Bradon Forest, **Somerford Forest** (permit only, W.T.N.C.) was clear-felled in the 1950s but is now managed to provide a great range of woodland variation. Ground flora include Primrose, Cowslip and their hybrid Oxlip, with a number of orchids.

Others: Peppercombe Wood (permit only, W.T.N.C.), Roundway Hill Covert Countryside Trail (SU 005647), Tanner's Wood (SU 033373).

Yorkshire and North Humberside

An area more renowned for its barren uplands and dales, Yorkshire nevertheless has a few woods worthy of a local visit. Common woodland birds abound at **Forge Valley Woods** (SE 985860). Oak, ash and elm provide the cover for hazel, Holly, Hawthorn, elder and Rowan and the under storey of Primroses, Bluebell, Wood Sorrel and Early Purple Orchid. **Grass Wood** (permit only, Yorkshire Wildlife Trust, Y.W.T.) grows on a steep limestone slope and has an under storey comprising Bluebell, Lily-of-the-valley, ferns and white-flowered Glossy Privet. A typical range of woodland birds can be seen. **Hetchell Wood** (permit only, Y.W.T.) is an alder swamp which supports populations of Dog's mercury, ramsons and Sanicle, with less frequent species such as Common Spotted Orchid and Greater Tussock Sedge. **Little Beck Wood** (permit only, Y.W.T.) is chiefly oak, ash and alder over a hazel, Holly, Rowan and Wych Elm under storey. Here in spring Bluebell, Wood Anenome and Early Purple Orchid can be seen, with a range of typical woodland birds, including Green Woodpecker, Marsh Tit, Woodcock and Dipper.

Others: Colt Park Wood (permit only, N.C.C.), Garbutt Wood (permit only, Y.W.T.), Hayburn Wick (permit only, Y.W.T.), Ling Gill (SD 803778), Moorlands (permit only, Y.W.T.), Sandall Beat (SE 610044), Stoneycliffe Wood (permit only, Y.W.T.).

WALES

Clwyd

Coed Cilygroeslyd. Permit only. 4ha. North Wales Naturalists' Trust (N.W.N.T.). Oak and ash form this woodland with an under storey of hazel, Hawthorn and Holly. Other sections contain dense thickets of Yew and beneath these there is little ground cover. In the more open sections carpets of Woodruff, Ivy, mosses and ferns grow. Interesting plants here include Stinking Hellebore, Greater Butterfly Orchid and Giant Bellflower. Pied Fly-catchers, several tit species and Green Woodpeckers prey on an abundance of insects in the wood and Tawny Owls hunt the many small mammals by night. Other predators include Fox, Stoat, and Weasel and very occasionally the rare Polecat. Typical woodland birds can also be seen from **Ewloe Castle Nature Trail** (SJ 292670). Here in spring fine spreads of Primroses and Bluebells can also be seen, whilst at **Hofod's Wood** (SJ 324477) the under storey comprises Wild Daffodil and Wood Spurge under a good range of native trees. Other parts of this woodland are open alder wetland with a ground flora of Great Horsetail, Hemlock, water dropwort and guelder rose. Here too the typical range of woodland birds can be seen including Spotted Flycatcher, the woodpeckers and Tawny Owl.

Others: Bishop's Wood Nature Trail (SJ 068813), Loggerhead's Country Park (SJ 198626), Tan-y-Cut Nature Trail (SH 282411).

Dyfed

The ash and Wych Elm of **Castle Woods** (SN 627220) form one of the finest wood-lands in this part of Wales. Oaks, beech, Wild Cherry and Holly also occur over a ground flora of spindle and Early Dog-violet. More specialized species such as

Toothwort also occur. Badgers and Foxes are common in the area which also holds a fine range of woodland birds including all three woodpeckers with Nuthatch, Tree-creeper, Sparrowhawk and Buzzard. The site is also noted for its fine lichen. Over sixteen species of fern occur at **Clettwr Valley** (permit only, West Wales Natural-ists Trust, W.W.N.T.). These include Rusty-back, Oak and beech Fern and both of our filmy ferns. The Pied Flycatcher, a bird to be found in many of these woodlands, occurs at **Coed Penglanowen** (permit only, W.W.N.T.) along with Spotted Fly-catcher and Sparrowhawk. The steep, oak woodland of **Coed Rheidol** (permit only, N.C.C.) contains Sanicle, Globe Flower, and Welsh Poppy, as well as a fine range of ferns, mosses, liverworts, and lichens. Fur-ther ferns can be seen at **Gwenffrwd-Dinas** (SN 787470) where the Hard, Oak, lemon scented, Lady and polypody fern and Wilson's Filmy Fern grow. Here too, Pied Flycatchers flit amongst the oak and birch of this steep valley woodland. However, the speciality of this reserve is the Red Kite which occurs with other avian predators such as Buzzard, Kestrel, Sparrowhawk and Tawny Owl. Wood Horsetail, Royal Fern and Globe Flower grow under oak, Sycamore, birch and rowan at **Nant Melin** (permit only, W.W.N.T.). The largest block of primary oak woodland left in the area can be seen at **Pengelli Forest** (SN 124395). Two types of woodland occur here, one dry and one wet, having a fine range of ground species including Common Cow-wheat, Heather, Bilbury, Tufted Hair-grass, Wood-ruff, Opposite-leaved Golden Saxifrage and Marsh Violet. The uncommon Polecat occurs with Fox, Badger and Rabbit. Birds include Pied Flycatcher, Redstart, Wood Warbler and Buzzard.

Others: Allt Rhyd-y-Groes (permit only, N.C.C.), Clettwr Valley (permit only, W.W.N.T.), Coed Llwyngorres (SN 100390), Coed-y-Castell (SN 667193), Coed-y-Tyddyn Du (SN 272426), Y Goyalt (permit only,

W.W.N.T.), Llanerch Alder Carr (permit only, W.W.N.T.), Old Warren Hill (SN 615787), Pendery Oak Wood (SN 550732).

Glamorgan

Berry Wood (permit only, Glamorgan Naturalists Trust, G.N.T.) is mainly of oak, but Crab Apple and Aspen also occur. This unpolluted wood holds fine examples of lichens, mosses and ferns which include Narrow Bucklerfern. Greater Spotted and Green Woodpecker occur with Pied Flycatcher and Woodcock at **Coed-y-Bedw Reserve** (permit only, G.N.T.), along with seventeen species of butterfly, a rich range of lichens, mosses and ferns and a host of ground flora which includes Traveller's Joy, Lousewort, Heath Bedstraw and Alpine Clematis. At **Coed-y-Bwl** (permit only, G.N.T.), you can see in spring a fine show of Lesser Celandine, Wild Daffodil, Wood Anemone, and Bluebell, under elm, ash and Field Maple. **Gelli Hir Wood** (permit only, G.N.T.), is very wet and acid and supports many different woodland habitats. Here Sparrowhawk, Tawny Owl, and Buzzard breed with a host of moths and butterflies, several of which are uncommon in the area. These include Silverwashed Fritillary and Holly Blue. The rare Purple Gromwell, a trailing and creeping plant with rich blue flowers, can be seen at **Porth Kerry Country Park** (ST 092672) in Cliff Wood, a typical limestone woodland of oak and ash growing over a coppice of hazel, Hawthorn and Yew. Other plants include Wild Madder and Traveller's Joy. **Taf Fechan** (SO 045097) is a steep wooded valley of oak, ash, and Sycamore. The under storey is of lime, beech, Bird Cherry and Dogwood reflecting the limestone substrate. Ground flora includes Fairy Flax, Wild Thyme, Common Birdsfoot Trefoil and Quaking Grass. The stream supports Dipper and Kingfisher whilst Raven, Buzzard and Sparrowhawk breed along with Nuthatch, Treecreeper,

two woodpeckers and Wood Warblers.
Others: Afan Argoed Country Park (SS 821951), Bishop's Wood (SS 594878), Cwm Risca (SS 881843), Amerley Wood (permit only, G.N.T.), Ilston Quarry, (permit only, G.N.T.), Margam Country Park (SS 813849), Oxwich (SS 501865), Peel Wood (permit only, G.N.T.), Wenallt Woods (ST 153831).

Gwent

Yellow Bird's-nest and Bird's-nest Orchid grow at **Cwm Clydach** (permit only, N.C.C.), under a dense canopy of beech growing here at its western limit. Oak, Wych elm, Downy Birch, Holly and Yew also grow with other ground plants, including scaly Male Fern, Bilberry and Hard Fern. Ancient woodlands can be found on the steep slopes of the lower Wye valley where oak and beech grow with a characteristic acid-loving ground flora. Elsewhere along the valley limestone woods contain ash, Wych Elm and Field Maple, and here the ground flora includes Dog's Mercury, Yellow Archangel, Bluebell, ramsons and Woodruff with Heart's Tongue and Soft Shieldfern. Lime-loving species include Marjoram, Ploughman's Spikenard, Yellow Bird's-nest, Wood Cranesbill, Wood Fescue, Mountain Melick and Thin-spiked Wood Sedge. Upright Spurge grows here and nowhere else in Britain. The rich variety of the ground flora gives rise to a fine range of butterflies, numbering almost half of the British species, including Holly Blue, Silver-washed Fritillary, and Speckled Wood. The rare Greater Horseshoe Bat roosts in riverside cliffs, and a typical range of woodland birds can be found throughout the valley. At **Old Church Wood** (permit only, Glamorgan Naturalists' Trust, G.N.T.) part of the lower Wye valley a superb spread of Wild Daffodil can be seen in spring. In **Wentwood Forest** (ST 436936), areas of beech and oak wood land remain amongst newly planted conifers. Here Broad-leaved Helleborine, Adder's Tongue and Wild Daffodil grow. A fine range of woodland breeding birds occurs, including Redstart and Wood Warbler, Buzzard and Sparrowhawk and both Dormouse and Harvest Mouse have been recorded.

Others: Black Cliff Wynd Cliff Forest (permit only, F.C.). Coed-y-Bwynydd (SD 365068), Cwm Coed-y-Cerrig (permit only, Brecon Beacons National Park Committee), Ladypark Wood (permit only, N.C.C.), Stain Mary's Vale Nature Trail (SD 283162), Strawberry Cottage Wood (permit only, G.N.T.), Ysg Yryd Fawr (SO 330180).

Gwynedd

Coed Camlyn (permit only, N.C.C.), **Coed Cymerau** (permit only, N.C.C.) and **Coed Dinorwig** (SH 586603) are three oak woodlands which have been ungrazed for many years. Under these small oaks Heather, Bilberry and Bramble grow, whilst in damper areas Great Wood-rush flourishes. They provide a sheltered dampness and encourage a good range of ferns, mosses and lichens. Species include Lady, Hard and Parsley Fern, Wilson's Filmy Fern, and Maidenhair Spleenwort. Such woodland is also a fine habitat for the Pied Flycatcher due to its richness in insect fauna. Buzzard, Kestrel and Sparrowhawk also occur. **Coed Dolgarrog** (permit only, N.C.C.) and **Coed Gorswen** (permit only, N.C.C.) are richer than most other woods in Gwynedd, and are comprised of oak, Wych Elm, ash, Small-leaved Lime and Crab Apple. The under flora consists of Dog's Mercury and Enchanter's Nightshade with Sanicle, Ramsons, Wild Strawberry and Common Dog-violet. Less common species include Moonwort and Broad-leaved Helleborine. The mixed valley woodland at **Coed Ydd Aber** (SH 662720) has a great range of ecotypes. Dry acid oak woodland on the higher slopes, varies to ash, Wych Elm and birch on the lower areas where Primrose, Bluebell, Wood Anenome and Wood Sorrel flower in spring. In wetter areas Creeping Buttercup and Opposite-leaved Golden Saxifrage occur. An excellent area for lichens, this wood holds a number of important rarities, as well as good breeding populations of Pied Flycatcher, Redstart and Wood Warbler and a range of other typical woodland birds. **Coedydd Maentwrog** (SH 652414) occurs in three woodland blocks. The trees are mostly oak which cover the fine range of ferns, mosses, and lichens. Flowering plants occur such as Common Cow-wheat, Primrose, Lesser Celandine and Common Dog-violet. Birds include Pied Flycatcher, Nuthatch, Treecreeper, two woodpeckers and Buzzard.

Others: Abercorris (permit only, N.W.N.T.), Bron-y-Graig Nature Trail (SH 583311), Cader Idris (SH 730114), Coed Llechwedd (SH 592318), Coed Lletywalter (SH 602275), Coed Twddyn Badyn (SH 565668), Coed-y-Rhygen (permit only, N.C.C.).

Powys

Nant Sere Wood (permit only, Brecon Naturalists' Trust, B.N.T.) set in the Brecon Beacons includes a diverse range of wet and damp woodland amongst grassland and scrub. Alder is the dominant tree, although oak, Holly and Field Maple also grow, as well as an area of ash. Wood Foxglove, Common Dog-violet, and Herb Robert grow with Bluebell and Yellow Pimpernel. Much of the wood is very damp and boggy; this provides for many ferns and mosses with a good range of liverworts and fungi. Birds are typical of lowland woods, and include Wood Warbler, Pied Flycatcher and several species of tit. **Pwll-y-Wrach** (SO 163327) is a tall oak wood above an under storey of ash, birch, Hawthorn, hazel and Spindle. Again this wood is rich with liverworts, mosses and ferns, the ground being very damp. Bluebell, Wood Sorrel, Woodruff, Dog's Mercury, Enchanter's Nightshade and Wild Strawberry, all grow on the wooded floor whilst Dipper, Grey and Pied Wagtail nest on the stream running at the bottom of the wood.

Others: Cefn Cenarth (permit only, H.R.N.T.), Coed Pendugwm (permit only, N.T.N.C.), Craig Irfon (permit only, B.N.T.), Lake Vyrnwy (SH 985215).

SCOTLAND

Borders

Beech, oak, ash and poplar dominate the woodland at **Dun's Castle** (NT 778550). This woodland is most exciting in spring when large areas are carpeted by Bluebells, ramsons, Red Campion, Purple Wood Cranesbill, Meadowsweet and Foxglove. Other less well-known woodland plants include Toothwort, Common Twayblade and the waxy-flowered Common Wintergreen. Badger, Roe Deer and Red Squirrel share the woodland with a fine range of woodland birds including Marsh Tit, breeding Pied Flycatcher, and a host of warblers. The many rides support a thriving insect population including several localized butterfly species. At **Gordon Moss** (permit only, Scottish Wildlife Trust, S.W.T.) the lichen-covered jungle of birch, willow, alder and Aspen supports many interesting plants. Coralroot Orchid, Lesser Butterfly Orchid, Lesser Wintergreen, Moonwort and Greater Spearwort all grow with a profusion of other floral interest. The site is also noted for its moths which include Small Chocolate Tip, Powdered Quaker and Beautiful Carpet. Small Pearl-bordered Fritillaries also occur.

Central

In spring carpets of ramsons, celandine Wood Sorrel and Dog's Mercury carpet the floor of **Doller Glen** (NS 9690). In summer the woods here support a fine range of woodland birds including Wood Warbler Spotted Flycatcher and four tit species Oak is the dominant tree but also some ash, Wych Elm and Sycamore occur. The islands on **Loch Lomond** (NS 3598) support a fine Sessile Oak forest with alder and ash in the wetter areas. Beneath the oaks wood-rush dominates with some Maidenhair Spleenwort, Woodruff, Dog's Mercury and Sanicle. The insect diversity is large and this supports a similarly large population of birds, including Wood, Willow and Garden Warblers, Redstart, Tree Pipit and Great Spotted Woodpecker. Similar woodland can be found at **Queen Elizabeth Forest Park** running along the banks of Loch Lomond. Under the oaks, Lesser Celandine, Bluebell, Dog's Mercury and Wood Sorrel flower amongst the jumble of mossy mounds and Bilberry humps. Also running along the banks of Loch Lomond is the **West Highland Way** (NS 896744 – NN 113743).

Dumfries and Galloway

Willow tits flourish at **Fountainbleau and Ladypark** (permit only, S.W.T.), where many decaying birch stumps are present for their nesting sites. The woodland is frequently flooded despite a network of drainage ditches. As a result its wetness leads to large numbers of fungi, liverworts and mosses. Ground flora includes Marsh Cinquefoil, Marsh Pennywort, Marsh Thistle, Woody nightshade and Water-pepper. Birds include Sedge Warbler, Reed Bunting and Redpole. Mammals include Water Shrew living in the drainage ditches and Roe Deer. A small area of mature oakwood can be found at **Kendey Marshes** (NX 636869), where Pied Flycatcher and Wood Warbler breed and two woodpecker species occur.

Grampian

Semi-natural oak-wood can be found at **Dinnet Oakwood** (NO 464980) which is one of the few remaining such woods in north-east Scotland. Ground flora include Chickweed Wintergreen, Common Wintergreen and Stone Bramble. A typical range of woodland birds is present; Wood Warbler, Spotted Flycatcher, Jay and Great Spotted Woodpecker among them. Several uncommon insects occur in the wood, which is of both Sessile and Pendunculate Oak. Some deciduous woodland can be found in the middle Deeside area amongst other mixed and fully coniferous blocks. Here some fine old oaks occur, probably dating from the early nineteenth century, that were once coppiced. These are supported with a good range of woodland birds, including Green Woodpecker, Jay, Buzzard, Goshawk and in some areas, Woodcock.

Highland North

At **Allt Nan Carnan** (NG 8940) oak and birch dominate the woodland with Bird Cherry, ash, Rowan, Holly and hazel. A fine range of bryophytes is present with a ground flora of Stone Bramble, Yellow Saxifrage, Opposite-leaved Golden Saxifrage and Alpine Lady's Mantle. **Drummondereach** (permit only, S.W.T.) has a very rich ground flora suggesting that this replanted woodland stands on an original old oak-wood site. Ash, Rowan and birch also now occur, over Herb Paris, Moschattle, Enchanter's Nightshade, Meadow Cow-wheat and Hard Shieldfern. Remnants of birch and hazel woodland can be found at **Inverpolly** (NC 1312). Birch now dominates the woodland with some hazel and Rowan. Holly, oak and Bird Cherry can also be found. The underflora consists of Self-heal, Primrose, Common Dog Violet, Meadowsweet and a variety of mosses, liverworts and lichens. Lemon Scented fern and Wilson's Filmy fern are also abundant in some places. Badgers can be found and here they live in holes in the rocks rather than in excavated setts. A very northerly ash-wood containing hazel and some Rowan, Blackthorn and Hawthorn can be found at **Rassle Ash Wood** (NG 8443). Ground flora can only be found in fenced enclosures or on the sides of the gorge where they are protected from the local sheep, but many lichens of particular interest can be found growing on the trees or the boulders on the woodland floor.

Highland South

At **Craigellachie** (NH 8812) a fine open birch woodland can be explored. Both Silver and Downy Birch are present in the woods with Rowan, aspen, hazel, oak and Bird Cherry. Ground flora includes a good range of ferns, lichen and fungi, but grasses and mosses dominate the ground vegetation with Common Rock-rose, Alpine Bistort and Alternate-leaved Golden Saxifrage sometimes occurring. Birds include several tit species, Great Spotted Woodpecker, Woodcock, Treecreeper and Willow Warbler. Several locally uncommon moth species occur, such as the Rannock Sprawler, Kentish Glory and Angle Stripped Sallow. Another birch-dominated woodland can be found at **Farigaig** (permit only, S.W.T.). Here the ground flora is predominantly Heather and Bilberry but some other species such as Common Wintergreen can be found. An abundance of leafy liverworts, mosses and lichens can be found in the oak woodlands at **Loch Sunnart** (NM 8464 – 6558). This old coppice also has some birch, hazel and Rowan.

Lothian

Pepperwood (permit only, S.W.T.), is noted for its Lily-of-the-valley, Leopard's-bane, Butterburr and heart leaved Valerian, but the wood holds most common native woodland plants. Oak, ash and Wych Elm occur with fourteen other broad-leaved species at **Rossling Glyn** (permit only, S.W.T.). Here Honeysuckle abounds and provides cover for woodland birds, such as Wood Warbler, Redstart and Pied Flycatcher. Ground flora includes Dog's Mercury, Wood Anemone, Woodruff and ramsons. The woodland is also rich in bryophytes. Both Red and Grey Squirrel are found on this reserve as are Badger and Fox. **Thornton Glen** (permit only, S.W.T.) has probably been untouched for several hundred years. The woods here are pre-

dominantly ash, elm, Holly and hazel and seven species of fern are present with many bryophytes species.

Skye and other Islands

Birch and hazel woodland with some Rowan, willow, ash, and oak can be found at **Clan Donald Centre** (NG 6105) with Herb Robert, Lesser Twayblade, Stone Bramble and Melancholy Thistle amongst the ground floral interest. Roe Deer can be found with the typical variety of woodland birds. On Eigg some hazel scrub-woodland can be explored. Here ferns flourish including Lemon Scented Fern, Broad and Narrow Bucklerfern and scaly Male Fern. Typical woodland ground flora such as Wood Sorrel, Wood Anemone, ramsons, Wood Sage and Wild Strawberry occur with Yellow Pimpernel and huge patches of Bluebell which extend beyond the woodland over bracken-covered slopes. Two wooded ravines can be found at **Laig Farm**, and here Heart's Tongue Fern and Wilson's Filmy Fern are among the plants growing in the deep shade of the ravines. **Tokavaig Wood** (NG 6112) is a relict piece of semi-natural woodland, ash being the dominant species with some hazel and Bird Cherry. Again noted for its bryophytes, lichens and ferns, a typical ground flora can be found in this very humid mixed woodland.

Strathclyde North

Semi-natural woodland still survives in small parts of the **Argyll Forest Park**. Oak dominates the woods with ash, hazel, birch and alder, over a ground flora of Primroses, Bluebells, Wood Anemone and violets in spring. The mild climate and high rainfall again leads to a rich abundance of ferns, mosses, liverworts and lichens. A typical range of woodland birds can be found. **Glasdrum Woods** (NN 0545) is comprised of alder, ash and hazel over a rich ground flora including a variety of ferns amongst Dog's Mercury, Wood Anemone and Enchanter's Nightshade. Again it is rich in bryophytes and lichen species. **Glen Nant** (NN 0128) is a native deciduous woodland with stumps of coppiced oak over 400 years old. Ash, hazel and birch now grow with Bird Cherry, Rowan and Holly over a ground flora in some places dominated by ferns. Oak Fern, Lemon Scented fern, Hay-scented Bucklerfern, scaly Male Fern and Wilson's Filmy Fern are among the species found amongst a luxuriant growth of mosses. Birds include Wood Warbler, Redstart and Great Spotted Woodpecker. Mammals include Roe Deer and Hedgehogs, whilst the butterflies include Dark Green Fritillary and Green-veined White. The largest remaining remnant of oak-woods in this part of Scotland occurs at **Tannish** (NR 7384) where a verdant growth of mosses carpets the boulders on the woodland floor. Scotch Argus butterflies are common in late summer and as with all of these woodland types lichens, bryophytes and mosses are common.

Strathclyde South

Brodick Country Park (NS 0138) contains mature specimens of oak and beech over a damp ground flora, including mosses, liverworts, lichens and ferns, whilst at **Clyde Valley Woodlands** (NS 9045) a diverse woodland cover of elm, ash, oak and alder supports a typical range of ground plants, including Rough Horsetail, Wood Fescue, Herb Paris and Stone Bramble. **Enterkine Wood** (permit only, S.W.T.) has sixteen broad-leaved tree species, many of which were planted but natural regeneration is now occurring. A typical range of woodland birds occurs, with thirty-four species breeding, among these Blackcap, Goldfinch and Woodcock. Ground flora includes large areas of Blue grouse, Wood Anemone, Enchanter's Nightshade and Dog's Mercury. A remote woodland remnant can be found at **Glen Diomhan** (NR 9246) where two native species of whitebeam, both restricted to north Arran can be found. Common Spotted Orchid, Lesser Butterfly Orchid, Meadowsweet, valerian and Purple Loosetrift are among the typical plants to be found on a thin strip of oak, birch and beech woodland running through **Loch Winnock Reserve** (NS 3558).

Tayside

A variety of ferns grow amongst the rocks and moss-covered tree trunks at **Killiecrankie** (permit only, R.S.P.B.). The oak-dominated woodland holds Wood Warbler, Redstart, Green Woodpecker, Great Spotted Woodpecker, Buzzard, Kestrel and Raven. Ground plants include Wood Vetch, Yellow Saxifrage and Shining Cranesbill. Oak and beech dominate the woods at **Linnof Tummell** (NN 9160) with hazel, birch and alder. The underflora includes Wood Melick, Stone Bramble, Primrose, Common Wintergreen, Lily-of-the-valley and Common Dog-violet. Bilberry and Heather can also be found in profusion. Birds include Siskin, Redpoll, Long-tailed Tit and Treecreeper. Roe Deer and Red Squirrel are also common. Nearby the **Tummell Forest** (NN 865597) has steep slopes of mixed deciduous woodland over Dog's Mercury, Wood Anemone, Wood Sorrel, Marsh Hawksbeard, Climbing Corydalis, and Broad Bucklerfern. Here Redstart, Wood Warbler and Spotted Flycatcher breed.

SOME USEFUL ADDRESSES

British Dragonfly Society
c/o The Secretary
4 Peakland View
Darley Dale
Matlock
Derbyshire DE4 2GF

British Herpetological Society
c/o Zoological Society of London
Regents Park
LONDON NW1 4RY

British Trust for Ornithology
Beech Grove
Tring
Hertfordshire HP23 5NR

Forestry Commission
(South East and New Forest)
The Queens House
Lyndhurst
Hampshire SO4 7NH

Nature Conservancy Council
Northminster House
Peterborough PE1 1VA

Royal Society for Nature Conservation
The Green
Nettleham
Lincoln LN2 2NR

Royal Society for the Protection of Birds
The Lodge
Sandy
Bedfordshire SG19 2DL

The Woodland Trust
Westgate
Grantham
Lincolnshire NG31 6LL

THE PHOTOGRAPHS

All the photographs in this book were taken using 35 mm SLR Canon Cameras (A-1 and F-1) in conjunction with the following Canon FD lenses; 28mm, 50mm, 70–210mm zoom, 100mm macro and 500mm F8 reflex. They were all taken using Kodakchrome 64 slide film using a tripod and cable release. In some cases filters have been used, (primarily 81B, softener and polarizing) to enhance or destroy some aspect of the reality.

LEFT **Ravaged bark**

BIBLIOGRAPHY

Allaby, M. *The Woodland Trust Book of British Woodlands.* David and Charles, London, 1986.

Andrewes, Sir Christopher. *The Lives of Wasps and Bees.* Chatto and Windus, London, 1969.

Brooks, M. and **Knight, C.** *A Complete Guide to British Butterflies.* Jonathan Cape, London, 1982.

Brown, L. *British Birds of Prey.* Collins New Naturalist, London, 1976.

Carter, D. *Butterflies and Moths of Britain and Europe.* Pan, London, 1982.

Carroll, L. *The Complete Lewis Carroll.* Penguin Books, Harmondsworth, England, 1982.

Chapman, D. and **A.** *Fallow Deer, Their History, Distribution and Biology.* Terence Dalton Ltd., Lavenham, Suffolk, 1975.

Chinery, M. *A Field Guide to the Insects of Britain and Northern Europe.* Collins, London, 1972.

Corbet, G. B. and **Southern, H. N. (Eds.).** *The Handbook of British Mammals,* (2nd Ed.). Blackwell Scientific Publications, Oxford, England, 1977.

Cramp, S. and **Simmons, K. E. L. (Eds.).** *Handbook of the Birds of Europe, the Middle East and North Africa.* The Birds of the Western Palearctic (7 volumes – 4 published). Oxford University Press, 1977.

Dale, J. E. *The Growth of Leaves.* Institute of Biology Reader Nos. 137. Edward Arnold, London, 1982.

Davies, P., Davies, J. and **Huxley, A.** *Wild Orchids of Europe.* Chatto and Windus, London, 1983.

Etherington, R. *Plant Physiological Ecology.* Institute of Biology Reader Nos. 98. Edward Arnold, London, 1978.

Eyre, S. R. *Vegetation and Soils, A World Picture.* Edward Arnold, London, 1968.

Ford, E. B. *Butterflies.* Collins New Naturalist, London, 1945.

Frazer, D. *Reptiles and Amphibians.* Collins New Naturalist, London, 1983.

Gibbons, B. *Dragonflies and Damselflies of Britain and Northern Europe.* Country Life/Hamlyn, London, 1986.

Goodden, R. *British Butterflies. A Field Guide.* David and Charles, Newton Abbott, 1978.

Harrison, C. *A Field Guide to the Nests, Eggs and Nestlings of British and European Birds.* Collins, London, 1975.

Heinzel, M., Fitter, R. and **Parslow, J.** *The Birds of Britain and Europe with North Africa and the Middle East.* Collins, London, 1972.

Higgins, L. G. and **Riley, N. D.** *A Field Guide to the Butterflies of Britain and Europe.* Collins, London, 1970.

Hywel-Davies, J. and **Thom, V. (Eds.).** *The Macmillan Guide to Britain's Nature Reserves.* Macmillan, London, 1984.

Jackson, J. *Deer in the New Forest.* Moonraker Press, Bradford-on-Avon, 1977.

Jones, D. *The Country Life Guide to Spiders of Britain and Northern Ireland.* Country Life/Hamlyn, London, 1983.

Lack, P. *The Atlas of Wintering Birds in Britain and Ireland.* T. & A. D. Poyser, Calton, England, 1986.

Linssen, E. F. *Beetles of the British Isles* (2 volumes). Warne, London, 1959.

McClintock, D. and **Fitter, R. S. R.** *A Pocket Guide to Wildflowers.* Collins, London, 1956.

Neal, E. G. *Badgers.* Blandford Nocturnal Series. Blandford Press, Poole, 1977.

Newton, I. *The Sparrowhawk.* T. & A. D. Poyser, Calton, England, 1986.

Ovington, J. D. *Woodlands.* The English Universities Press Ltd., London, 1965.

Peterson, R., Mountfort, G. and **Hollom, P. A. D.** *A Field Guide to the Birds of Britain and Europe.* Collins, London, 1954 (Fourth Edition, 1983).

Phillips, R. *Wild Flowers of Britain.* Pan, London, 1977.

Phillips, R. and **Shearer, L.** *Mushrooms: and Other Fungi of Great Britain and Europe.* Pan, London, 1981.

Porter, R. F., Willis, I., Christensen, S. and **Nielsen, B. P.** *Flight Identification of European Raptors.* T. & A. D. Poyser, Berkhamstead, England, 1976.

Putman, R. J. and **Wratton, S. D.** *Principles of Ecology.* Croom Helm, London, 1984.

Ramsbottom, J. *Mushrooms and Toadstools.* Collins New Naturalist, London, 1953.

Reade, W. and **Hoskins, E.** *Nesting Birds, Eggs and Fledglings in Colour.* Blandford, London, 1967.

Ridpath, I. *Guide to Stars and Planets.* Collins, London, 1984.

Sharrock, J. T. R. *The Atlas of Breeding Birds in Britain and Ireland.* T. & A. D. Poyser, Berkhamstead, England, 1976.

South, R. *The Moths of the British Isles* (2 volumes). Warne, 1961.

Spradbury, J. P. *Wasps.* Sidgwick and Jackson, London, 1973.

Streeter, D. and **Gerrard, I.** *The Wildflowers of the British Isles.* Macmillan, London, 1983.

Sutton, S. L. *Woodlice.* Ginnard Company Ltd., London, 1972.

Tensley, A. G. *Britain's Green Mantle, Past, Present and Future.* George Allen and Unwin, London, 1949.

Whalley, P. *Butterfly Watching.* Severn House Naturalist Library, London, 1980.

Figures in bold type refer to
photographs (often with text relating to
species on same page); figures in italics
refer to colour paintings.

LEFT **The mossy woodland floor**
RIGHT **The green mosaic**